Vocabular **...** **ix**

Understanding, Learning, Teaching

Michael McCarthy

Anne O'Keeffe

Steven Walsh

Australia • Brazil • Japan • Korea • Mexico • Singapore • Spain • United Kingdom • United States

HEINLE
CENGAGE Learning

Vocabulary Matrix:
Understanding, Learning, Teaching
Michael McCarthy, Anne O'Keeffe
and Steven Walsh

Publisher: Jason Mann

Commissioning Editor: John Waterman

Development Editor: Eunice Yeates

Product Manager: Ruth McAleavey

Content Project Editor: Amy Smith

Manufacturing Manager: Helen Mason

Cover Designer: Adam Renvoize

Text Designer: Melinda Welch

Compositor: KGL

For permission to use material from this text or product,
submit all requests online at **cengage.com/permissions**

Further permissions questions can be emailed to
permissionrequest@cengage.com

ISBN: 978-1-4240-5253-0

Heinle, Cengage Learning EMEA
Cheriton House, North Way, Andover, Hampshire
SP10 5BE United Kingdom

Cengage Learning is a leading provider of customised learning
solutions with office locations around the globe, including
Singapore, the United Kingdom, Australia, Mexico, Brazil
and Japan. Locate our local office at:
international.cengage.com/region

Cengage Learning products are represented in Canada
by Nelson Education, Ltd.

Visit Heinle online at **elt.heinle.com**
Visit our corporate website at **cengage.com**

Photo credits
The publishers would like to thank the following sources for permission to reproduce their copyright protected
photographs:
3t (istock/blackred), 3br(a) (istock/Luca di Filippo), 3br(b) (istock/Francesco Rossetti), 3br(c) (istock/mbphoto),
14 (Eunice Yeates), 15 (JupiterImages), 17tl (istock/Emilia Stasiak), 17tr (istock/Morgan Lane Photography),
17bl (istock/Phocus), 17br (istock/Antonio Ovejero Diaz), 21 (istock/Janice Dreosti).

Printed in the United Kingdom by Lightning Source
Print Number 04 Print Year 2016

Contents

10 Words in society 113

Authors' preface

Our days are filled with thousands of words. We say them; we hear them; we read them; we write them and we think them. As teachers, they are our medium and they are our message. Even at the most elementary level of teaching, words are our starting point. Therefore, it is fundamentally important to stop and think about what words are, how they mean, how they relate to other words and how they function in different ways in society. This applies particularly in the case of English and, because of its global spread, new words come into being every day while old words are given new or additional meanings. We need to understand this process and to develop in our students an awareness of the dynamic nature of words, their meanings and their many uses.

This book leads the reader through the life story of a word. We bring you from the basics of word formation and on through how words have meanings. We look at how words form relationships with other words, how they inter-relate with grammar, how they attract one another and gather in groups (collocations, multi-word units and idioms), how they operate in spoken and written texts, how we learn them, how we teach them and how we use them, change them and recreate them in society. Our discussion is backed up by evidence from a large corpus (a computerised database of hundreds of millions of words of spoken and written English texts which we can search and analyse to see how the language is really used), as well as real data from the classroom.

Words are more than mere individual containers with meaning. They exist in a complex matrix which links them to morphemes (prefixes and suffixes), other meanings (synonyms, antonyms), other words (that is, the words that they are likely to occur with or be associated with), grammar patterns, multi-word units (groups of words that are fixed into phrases or idioms). This matrix extends well beyond the sentence to spoken and written texts and it also has both a cognitive and social dimension.

We have structured the book around ten chapters. Each chapter is divided into three parts: (A) What do we know about this?; (B) What are the problems for learners?; and (C) How do we teach it? Part A provides the background information and theory relating to each topic. Part B identifies the problems which learners will have in relation to this aspect of vocabulary and Part C provides a discussion of how we can apply the theory from Part A to our teaching and how we can address the challenges which are raised in Part B.

Throughout the book, we use tasks to contextualise the theoretical and pedagogical concepts which we cover. Many of these tasks may be adaptable for use with your learners, or, if you are a teacher trainer, for use with your trainees. We provide a commentary on these tasks either in the chapter or, in some cases, at the end of the book. At the end of each chapter, there is a ten-question review section; the answer key and review commentary are also provided at the end of the book. This will aid self-study and review. To further aid self-study, we provide a glossary of all key terms.

The ten chapters of the book are structured in such a way as to lead the reader from the specific to the general. We begin in Chapter 1 by asking the question: what is a word? We then look at how words are formed, how they are pronounced and stressed, how the vocabulary changes, and just how big the vocabulary of English is. This last question gives us some idea as to the size of the task for learners of English. We also consider the core vocabulary that is needed for everyday communication.

Chapter 2 looks at how words have meaning. The link between a word and its meaning is one of chance. Words are created by consensus within a given society. In this chapter, we explore the notion of words having more than one meaning (polysemy) and we look at the challenges this poses for learners and teachers. We introduce the concept of word relationships, such as words which have similar meanings (synonyms) or words which have opposite meanings (antonyms).

Chapter 3 focuses on collocation; that is, the likelihood of two or more words occurring together. Native speakers and expert users of English know more than just individual words: they know how words combine in pairs which regularly occur together. Collocation is part of the meaning of words, and we look at how we can use collocation to describe the meaning of common, everyday words. Collocation is likely to be a new concept for our students and we consider how it can be introduced in the class in different ways and at different levels.

Chapter 4 introduces the concept that words also have grammatical meanings. We cannot simply divide words into 'grammar' words and 'meaning' words. They are linked in grammatical patterns which we call colligations, for example, *in the middle of the night* but *in the dead of night* (no article). This poses a difficult challenge for learners. We suggest various ways in which they can work on the patterns of words so as to build up their awareness. We especially stress the importance of good vocabulary notebook strategies.

Chapter 5 looks at multi-words. When we start to describe words, we see that a 'word' can be represented in any number of ways. It can be a single item (such as *lamp*), a compound (such as *door-handle*), a lexical chunk with a relatively fixed meaning (for example, *you know what I mean*), or a prepositional phrase (such as *at the end of the day*). In this chapter, we look at the ways in which combinations of words function to produce specific meanings, focusing on compounds, prepositional phrases and lexical chunks.

Chapter 6 is about idioms, the colourful expressions whose meanings we cannot guess just from the words they contain (for example, *keep your nose to the grindstone, get out of hand*). Although idioms are not very frequent, they stand out and teachers and learners enjoy learning them. We look at different types of idioms and how people use them in communication to comment on events and situations. We consider what problems they present for learners, how they might be taught in class and how we might take learners from single words and collocations to these longer expressions.

In Chapter 7 we look in greater detail at the relationships which words form with other words. We cover the advantages and disadvantages of relying on these relationships when teaching meaning. For example, what are the challenges of teaching meaning through synonyms and anonyms? What about using the words that are the same in your language and in English (cognates)? Are some of these actually false friends?

Chapter 8 explores words in text and discourse. By looking at longer stretches of texts, we can learn a lot about their internal structure and organisation. When we look at words in continuous texts, or discourse, we see that they play a key role in creating a sense of order. Words in spoken and written discourse perform important functions which help speakers and writers establish meanings with their audience. In this chapter, we look at lexical cohesion, lexical chains, stance and register.

Chapter 9 deals with words in the mind. We are interested in the ways in which we store, retrieve and use vast quantities of words and in the processes which enable us to do this relatively quickly and easily. Any discussion which looks at words in the mind, or our mental lexicon, is based on partial understandings since we cannot see how the mind works. Instead, we will use observations of how language is used and how we behave with language as a means of understanding how words are stored and retrieved.

Chapter 10 takes a broad look at words in society. We explore how words come into and go out of use and how they are used in different registers. We look at how new words are actually created and we question whether most of these are in fact new words or just combinations of words that we already know (*chick lit – chick + literature*) or old words put to new uses (for example, *to surf the Internet*). The media, the Internet and popular culture are discussed as influential forces on English and the spread of new words and patterns. We look at how words have particular associations and connotations and social restrictions on their use. We discuss the challenges which this ever-changing language poses for learners and their teachers and suggest ways in which depth of vocabulary knowledge can be developed.

We hope you enjoy reading this book as much as we enjoyed writing it, and that it inspires you to read more about vocabulary and to improve your own understanding and teaching of English.

Michael McCarthy
Anne O'Keeffe
Steve Walsh

1 | Words and their forms

What is a word and how are words formed?

TASK 1

How many words are there on each line? Write in your answers, as in the examples.

car	1
car park	2
it's	
pre-school	
prejudge	
forgetful	

Vocabulary is all about words. When we use language we use words all the time, thousands of them. If we know a language well, we know how to write its words and how to say its words. However, it may surprise you to know that it is not all that easy to say exactly what a 'word' is. One way would be to say that a word represents one unit of meaning and, in writing, has a space either side of it. So it would seem easy enough, at least in writing, to know what a word is – something with a space on either side. Because of this, we can confidently say that in Task 1, above, *car park* consists of two written words. But what about *it's*? There is no space in the middle, but most of us would say that *it's* consists of two words, *it* and *is* (shortened using *'s*). English has a convention, or 'rule', of using the symbol' (the apostrophe) to show when a word has been shortened and joined to another word. Examples include:

Word	Full form	Example
I'll	I shall or I will	I'll help you.
We've	we have	We've finished.
She'd	she would or she had	She'd have come if she'd known.
He's	he is or he has	He's a teacher and he's worked in Japan.

We do this shortening to show in writing how we typically *say* these words. A written word has spaces on either side, so *we've* is one written word when we want to show how it is spoken in informal situations (*we've* finished) and two written words (*we have* finished) when we want to show how it is spoken in more formal situations. In speech, *we've* is one word, pronounced /wi:v/.

In Task 1, you may have had a problem deciding whether *pre-school* was one word or two, and you may have noticed two elements in *prejudge* (*pre* and *judge*), but still decided it was one word because there was no space. This is because, in English, words which have extra elements added on at the beginning to change their meaning (prefixes) are sometimes written as one continuous word, and sometimes written with a hyphen (-). Examples include:

With hyphen	Without hyphen
post-industrial	postgraduate
pre-existing	prehistoric
non-event	nonentity

Generally, we consider words that have prefixes to be just one word, whether written as a continuous single word or with a hyphen. And whether we write them with a hyphen or not, we always speak them as one word.

In the case of *forgetful* in Task 1, again, you can probably see the word *forget* and an extra piece of meaning (*-ful*), which changes the verb to an adjective (e.g. *a forgetful person*). Extra pieces of meaning added to the ends of words are called suffixes (the opposite of prefixes, which are added to the beginnings of words). Suffixes are usually written without spaces or hyphens, so a word with a suffix is just one word.

The process of making new words by adding prefixes and suffixes is called **derivation,** and words like *impossible, illegal, statement* and *explanation* are derived forms of *possible, legal, state* and *explain*, respectively.

The bits of meaning that we can see in words such as *statement* (state-ment) and *impose* (im-pose) are called **morphemes.** Some morphemes can stand alone; they are free and can be words in their own right, such as *state, pose*. But other morphemes can't stand alone; they are bound and must be attached to something else, such as *-ment* and *im-*. So, as well as knowing what words are and what they mean, we also have knowledge of how they are constructed internally. This can often help us understand words we are not familiar with, or new words we have not seen before. Most educated users of English, for example, would have a good chance of understanding the word *retro-fit*, which has recently become popular, because they know that the bound morpheme *retro-* means going back or looking back, and they know the verb *fit*, so the term probably means to make something fit better or properly in a situation where it already exists.

Words and lexical items

TASK 2

Now do the same as in Task 1. How many words are there on each line? Write in your answers.

waste paper basket	
desktop	
blog	
phone	
DVD	
look looks looking looked	

Figure 1.1

You probably (correctly) said in Task 2 that *waste paper basket* was three words. You also almost certainly know what the individual words *waste, paper* and *basket* mean separately. Yet we know that a waste paper basket is one single object in the real world (Figure 1.1). The same is true of *desktop*. We can see two words – *desk* and *top* – but you may have a computer which is a *desktop* computer, or you may call the computer screen where you store important files and shortcuts to useful programmes your *desktop*. But *desktop* is written as just one word, unlike *waste paper basket*.

So, although we might see two words in one, or two or three separate words in writing, they may just represent or mean one single thing. We call these **compound words.** They are separate words that have come together to form one item of meaning, or one lexical item. English has thousands of compound words. Examples include:

Lexical item	Written words	Meaning
laptop	1	thin, portable computer that you can use on your lap
sleepwalk	1	to walk around while you are asleep
car park	2	place where you can leave your car temporarily
memory stick	2	small external drive for storing computer data
ice cream cone	3	conical wafer which can be filled with ice cream
Commander-in-chief	3	highest rank in the armed forces

So, words – which are the single units of a language – can come together to form compound words, which have one meaning and become one lexical item.

In the case of *blog* in Task 2 above, you would be right in saying that it is one word. It is a relatively new word which came into popularity in the first decade of this century. It was actually created from two words, *web* and *log*; it is like a diary or logbook, but it is on the World Wide Web. In *blog*, only the 'b' of *web* remains; the two words, *web* and *log*, have fused together to form one word and one lexical item, and some sounds have been lost in the process. We call these words **blends.** Some examples of blends in English include:

Blend	Words combined
brunch	**br**eakfast and l**unch**
motel	**mo**tor (car) and **tel**
Spanglish	**Span**ish and En**glish**

In the case of *phone* in Task 2, above, you probably did not hesitate in saying it is one word. It is indeed one word, but it is a short form of a longer word, *telephone*. Sometimes words are cut shorter in this way, and this process is called **clipping.** In the process of clipping, part of a word is lost, but the meaning of the lexical item is not changed; it remains the same as the full word. Clippings in English include:

Clipping	Full word
gas	*gasoline*
flu	*influenza*
gym	*gymnastics*
maths	*mathematics*

DVD in Task 2, above, is an example of a way in which technical words are often composed. That is to say, long or difficult technical terms are reduced to their first letters and a word is formed just from the initials. *DVD* means 'digital versatile disc', but no-one ever says that; everyone says *D-V-D*. This process of **initialism** is common, and we see it in examples like *BBC* (British Broadcasting Corporation), *CIA* (Central Intelligence Agency), *WHO* (World Health Organisation), and so on. Sometimes the first letters of a string of words are pronounced like a whole new word; such words are called **acronyms.** Examples include *laser* (Light Amplification by Stimulated Emission of Radiations) and *radar* (Radio Detection And Ranging). Most people have either forgotten or never even knew where these words originally came from; they are now just 'words' like any other, and each one is just a single lexical item, even though several lexical items may have been involved originally.

Finally, in Task 2, above, we had *look, looks, looking* and *looked*, which are all separate words, but which we know to be different grammatical forms of the same verb, *look*. So we can say that there is just one lexical item, 'look', which has various word-forms (the base-form *look*; the third person present simple form *looks*; the *-ing* form *looking;* and the past tense and past participle form *looked*). The word-forms *looks, looking* and *looked* are inflections of the base form *look*. **Inflected forms** give us grammatical information about the way a word is being used in a sentence.

We have already considered the various ways in which words are formed as well as the difficulties in deciding where the boundaries of words apply and what elements make up a word, especially when they are shortened or joined together. But we also have to pronounce words when we speak them, and this too raises problems for a language like English.

Words and pronunciation

One problem with English is that the pronunciation of words is often not predictable. Notorious examples include words ending in *-ough*:

Word	Pronunciation
cough	/kɒf/ - rhymes with *off*
tough	/tʌf/ - rhymes with *buff*
though	/ðəʊ/ - rhymes with *go*
through	/θruː/ - rhymes with *you*
bough	/baʊ/ - rhymes with *now*

Other variations in pronunciation between words which have similar spellings include *put* versus *but*; *school* versus *foot*; *out* versus *route*; and *new* versus *sew*. People learning English, whether as a first or second language, have to become accustomed to this lack of fit between sound and spelling which affects so many words.

Another problem is that, when we say words together, either as compounds or one after another fairly quickly, the sounds change to make the words easier to pronounce. Here are some examples:

Words spoken together	Written word(s)
/ˈhæmˌbæg/	handbag
/ˈrisˌwɒtʃ/	wrist watch
/ˈmʌnsəˌgəʊ /	months ago
/ˌdjʊːˈwɒnsəm /	Do you want some?

In writing, it is usually easy to separate words because they have spaces between them. In everyday, natural, spoken language, it is often difficult to relate what we hear to what we know about writing and spelling. The spoken language is often just a stream of sounds. However, we can usually understand what people mean in context.

We also need to know where to put the stress in a word. We need to know that *possess* has the stress on *-ess*, but that *possible* has the stress on *poss-*. Sometimes things are complicated because the same word can have a different stress depending on how it is used grammatically, whether as a noun, adjective or verb:

Word	As a noun	As a verb	As an adjective
record	**re**cord	re**cord**	
perfect		per**fect**	**per**fect

In addition, we need to know where to put the stress in a compound – often on the first word, but not always:

car park

laptop

waste paper basket

Commander-in-chief

Words change

The world is always changing. We experience changes in our cultures and societies as well as in technology and ways of thinking, and words have to change too. Old words and old meanings disappear (see Chapter 2), and new words are formed. In fact, very few completely new words are formed out of nowhere. Most new items consist of existing words which acquire new meanings; compounds which bring together existing words, or derivations of existing words, or new blends, initials, acronyms and clippings, which we examined above. Every year in English, new lexical items come into being. Consider these examples of terms from the world of computers. No-one would have understood these items in their technical contexts 50 years ago:

dongle	drop-down menu	PDA
Bluetooth	drag-and-drop	USB
download	hard drive	online
mousepad	auto-recovery	software

Another way English increases its vocabulary is simply by borrowing from other languages. Here are some examples of words that have entered English through contact with other cultures.

Word	Origin
amok	Malay – 'berserk, gone crazy'
chalet	French – 'a cabin or alpine-style hut'
feng shui	Chinese – 'wind and water'
jumbo	Swahili – 'elephant'
junta	Spanish – 'board, committee, meeting'
ombudsman	Swedish – 'official who deals with complaints from citizens'

English has borrowed thousands of words from other languages over its long history, and this has had important effects on the language. Most of the words borrowed from other languages sooner or later become pronounced in an English way, and so it is not always possible to detect immediately where they came from. The other effect is that English often has two kinds of words for the same thing: words whose origin lies in northern Europe (the Nordic and Anglo-Saxon world) and words which came from further south (the Mediterranean world – French, Latin and Greek words). Often, the Greek or Latin word for something is considered more formal than the Anglo-Saxon word for the same thing. Examples include *commence* versus *start*, *ascend* versus *go up*, and *depart* versus *leave*.

How big is the vocabulary and how many words do speakers know?

TASK 3

Answer the following questions. Make a guess if you don't know.

1 How many words are there in English?
2 How many words does an educated native speaker of English *understand*?
3 How many words does a speaker of English need to be able to *use* to take part in everyday conversation?

We have already seen that defining a 'word' is not a simple matter, since many lexical items consist of more than one word, but, generally, we can get an insight into how big the vocabulary of a language is by basing our counts on the **headwords** in dictionaries (the headwords are the words at the beginning of each entry, the words which the definition or explanation refers to). You may have been surprised at just how many words are in a huge dictionary such as the *Oxford English Dictionary* (OED) (see the answers to Task 3 at the back of the book). Obviously, not all of the words in the OED are still used nowadays, and many of them are dialect words which are only used in particular regions of the English-speaking world. But even relatively smaller, advanced learners' dictionaries usually contain many tens of thousands of entries. The Collins COBUILD Advanced Dictionary (2009), for example, has more than 30 000 headwords and many thousands of examples sentences showing different meanings of the words. It may be more realistic, therefore, to ask the question: How many words are in normal circulation in written and spoken English nowadays, which a native speaker 'knows'? To answer this question, we can first look at what experts have said. Plag (2003: 4) gives a figure of 45 000–60 000 words – thankfully, considerably less than the contents of the OED! Crystal (2003: 426) estimated in excess of 50 000 words for an educated speaker's active vocabulary and about 75 000 for the number of words likely to be understood. Nation and Waring (1997) give a figure of around 20 000 word families, which sounds significantly lower. However, the notion of word families is different from individual words. A **word family** is a word and all its inflected and regular derived forms, so we need to increase Nation and Waring's total to about 30 000 individual words or more, depending on exactly what it is we count as a 'word'. Whichever set of figures we accept, it does seem that native speakers know tens of thousands of words.

However, during our everyday lives, we rarely encounter many of the words we know. So, which ones are we likely to meet on a day-to-day basis? One way of answering this question is to use a **corpus** (plural: corpora). A corpus is a database of texts stored on a computer (see O'Keeffe et al., 2006 for an introduction). These texts can be written (for example, newspapers, magazines, novels, Web pages) or spoken (for example, transcripts of conversations or of radio and TV shows). Nowadays, dictionary publishers use huge corpora; the COBUILD Bank of English Corpus, for example, has over six hundred million words of texts in its database (Collins COBUILD, 2009: xi). Dictionary writers can search their corpus to find out which words are used frequently and which words occur, say, only once in many millions of words. Leech et al. (2001: 9), for example, report that, in the 100 000 000-word British National Corpus (BNC), more than 500 000 word forms only occur three times or fewer, and only 124 000 word forms occur ten times or more.

VOCABULARY FILE

Most typical English corpora show that about 50–60 000 word-forms are in common, fairly frequent usage (based on the criterion of occurring 20 times or more per 100 000 000 words). It would seem, then, that the evidence points towards native- and expert-users of English having a command of perhaps 50 000 or so word-forms.

Nonetheless, the picture is not entirely straightforward. Whichever corpus we look at, some words are massively more common than others. O'Keeffe et al. (2006: 32) report that the 2000 most frequent word-forms in the Cambridge International Corpus account for 83 per cent of the entire corpus. In other words, these top 2000 forms are working much, much harder than all the other word-forms in the corpus. It seems we survive on a day-to-day basis with a small core of hard-working words and a much bigger number of low-frequency words. Another way of saying this is that most of the vocabulary is quite low-frequency.

Part A of this chapter has looked at English from the point of view of what its words are, how they are formed and how many there are, along with the allied question of what its native speakers and expert users do with them. But what about learners of English? Where do they fit into this picture?

PART B What are the problems for learners?

How many words can learners learn?

TASK 4

Make a list of four things from Part A of this chapter that we know about English vocabulary which could be problematic for learners of English as a second or foreign language.

Undoubtedly, one of the biggest problems for learners of English is the sheer size of the task of learning all the words that native speakers know and can use. Learning the grammar of English (tenses, articles, prepositions, word order, and so on) seems a relatively small and finite task in comparison. Even if a learner learnt more than 1000 word families a year, it would take ten years or more to get anywhere near Nation and Waring's estimate of 20 000 word families that native speakers can command. Luckily, most learners do not need to reach native-speaker standard. Also luckily, as we have seen, many of those 20 000 word families will be very rare indeed, and learners are unlikely to encounter them or need to use them.

A more modest target of 10 000 word families might seem better, but here too there are problems. O'Keeffe et al. (2006: 32) show that the more words you learn, the less you get back. The top 2000 words cover 83 per cent of all the texts in their corpus, but when the learner reaches, for example, 6000 words or more, each 2000 new words learnt from the list deliver less and less in terms of coverage of typical texts. What about 6000 words as a target? With the 6000 most frequent word-forms, a reader can expect to cover over 90 per cent of all the words in a typical text, according to O'Keeffe et al.'s (ibid) figures. Being able to understand more than 90 per cent of most spoken and written texts would seem to be a realistic target. Although comprehension is not complete, at least at that point the learner has enough understanding to be able to use the context to help them with the unknown words, use a dictionary to help with difficult new words, and use the text in class with a teacher as well as other resources. In this way, they can understand enough so that the task not completely de-motivating.

Six thousand words and 90 per cent comprehension of a text still means that about one in every ten words will be new, which is a heavy learning burden. However, there are many resources and supports that the learner can call on. If the learner can push the word comprehension level up to the top 10 000, then they will probably be near 95 per cent comprehension, and one in 20 new words seems far less daunting and de-motivating.

VOCABULARY FILE

Some exceptional adult learners can, in fact, reach vocabulary sizes not far off the levels of educated native speakers.

Cervatiuc (2008) reports vocabulary sizes for high achievers at university level for non-native English speakers averaging around 16 500 word families. So the task is big, but very high achievement is not impossible.

What other issues are there for learners?

Other big issues for learners include simply being able to recognise words. If you speak a language with a completely different system of forming and writing words, you may find it difficult to remember the exact forms of words you have learnt. Many Arabic-speaking learners of English, for example, have difficulty distinguishing between what you give someone on their birthday (*a present*) and where criminals are sent (*a prison*), because of the way words are formed and written in their own language (see Ryan and Meara, 1991).

Another set of problems is knowing when a group of words is a compound, separating out the words and (by extension) the lexical items from the stream of speech, as well as the problems of spelling, pronunciation and stress touched upon in Part A of this chapter. For example, how do you know where to put the stress in a word if you have only ever read it and never heard it spoken? In general, relating sound and spelling is likely to be a big problem, given the lack of fit between sound and spelling that affects so many English words.

Derived forms may also be a problem. In a study of more than 100 non-native university-level users of English, Schmitt and Zimmerman (2002) found it did not necessarily hold that if a learner knew one word-form in a word family, they would know all the rest. So, for example, knowing the word *forget* did not guarantee that learners would also know *forgetful*, *unforgettably*, and other derived forms. Learners did seem to learn noun and verb derivatives over time, but adjective and adverb derivatives were not so easily learnt and assimilated.

One final issue relates to what we said about the overlay of different vocabularies in English and how these can affect formality (Latin/Greek words versus Anglo-Saxon ones, for example) and register (how appropriate language is to the situation). How does the learner know whether a word is old-fashioned, formal, impolite, or technical? And what can we do about all these problems?

PART C How do we teach it?

What should we teach about words?

Given what we have learnt about English words and the problems they may raise for learners in Parts A and B of this chapter, what can a teacher do in the classroom, and what can learners do to increase their knowledge of words?

Nowadays, it is not very popular in many parts of the world to teach about word formation in English. Communicative methodologies, which stress using the language rather than learning about it, and the pressures of the curriculum may mean there is little motivation or time for learning about derivations and compounds. Most learners do learn the inflections of words (for example, the plural and the past tense) in the grammar lesson, but should we teach learners about derivation? Schmitt and Zimmerman's (2002) study (see previous section) certainly seems to suggest that we should. Learning the most common prefixes and suffixes, their meanings and how useful or productive they are (that is, how many new words once can form with them) could increase a learner's vocabulary very rapidly. The suffix *-er/-or*, for example, can be used with a great number of verbs to indicate a person who does something (*writer, reader, worker, adviser, repairer, driver, teacher, actor* and so on). Tasks involving practice with prefixes and suffixes may be found in McCarthy and O'Dell (1999) for elementary level, and McCarthy and O'Dell (2001) for upper intermediate level, and both books include compounds in their word-lists.

VOCABULARY FILE

Time set aside for teaching word formation is time well-spent. It not only increases learners' vocabulary, but increases their language awareness too, as they learn to see that acquiring a good vocabulary means more than just memorising lists of words and translations into their own language.

Clearly, too, it is important to teach learners to be sensitive to the different registers that words may belong to, whether formal or informal, technical or non-technical, and so on. Here, dictionary-training is probably the most useful strategy, as well as always approaching words in context. Good learners' dictionaries give lots of information about words, not just how to spell them and what they mean. The dictionary also gives pronunciation information, and a really good dictionary will give some indication of how common or how rare a word is, based on a corpus, and whether the word belongs to a special register such as technical language, newspaper language, or informal spoken language and so on. Setting learners tasks to find particular information in a dictionary will help them to use dictionaries more efficiently, as well as increasing their awareness of the importance of things like register and word-stress, and also which words are frequent and therefore important to learn.

How many words should we teach, and which ones?

We have seen how a corpus can show us that more or less the top 2000 words in English work much harder than all the others. This would seem to be a good reason to focus on learning those words as quickly as possible, using whatever methods are most efficient and which learners find most productive for them personally. Lists of the top 2000 words can be found in book form (see, for example, Leech et al., 2001, for the BNC), as well as on the Internet (do an online search for the BNC lemma list or the top 2000 words in English, for example), and the most frequent words are in-built in some recent graded materials (see McCarthy et al., 2005).

The first 2000 words are the core, or survival level, vocabulary which learners will need. Learning them will have several positive outcomes:

1 The learner will be able to read, write, speak and listen at an elementary level about everyday topics, with the help of some additional subject-specific vocabulary.

2 Since the first 2000 words are so frequent in texts, they will help and motivate learners to develop the skills they will need, as readers and listeners, to guess strange words in context and to ask for help when they cannot understand something in a real situation.

3 Dictionaries typically use the first 2000 to 2500 words as their 'defining vocabulary', that is, the words they use to define other words. If you know the first 2000 words, understanding definitions in dictionaries will be much easier and you will learn new words more quickly.

Beyond the top 2000 words, learning can either continue with general vocabulary, or can become increasingly focused to reflect learners' real needs. For example, the dictionary-makers who put together the *Macmillan English Dictionary for Advanced Learners* (Macmillan, 2002: x) identified a central vocabulary of around 7500 words which advanced learners should know, based on corpus frequency information, and gave these a special type-colour and a star-rating system in the dictionary so that learners can see immediately that they are key words. In an even more focused way, learners whose needs are academic English can focus on the 570-word-family Academic Word List (AWL), assembled by Averil Coxhead and available at her university webpage; you can find it by doing an Internet search using her name. Vocabulary learning does not need to be a bewildering process and, with the help of corpora, focused and graded learning can take place.

One final question is: How many words per lesson can learners reasonably expect to learn? On his website, Rob Waring suggests that good, efficient learning of words out of context, using memory techniques, can lead to the ability to absorb 30–40 words per hour. Even if the learner falls short of this, it would seem a good way of mastering the first 2000 words as quickly as possible. Waring also gives advice on exactly how such lists of words for de-contextualised learning should be given to learners; a quick Internet search using his name will bring you to his homepage.

Thirty to forty words per hour is probably an unrealistic target for many learners, for whom the classroom or textbook will be the main source of learning. For this reason, O'Dell and McCarthy, in their vocabulary teaching materials (for example, McCarthy and O'Dell, 1997; 2001) suggest around 15–18 words per one hour unit/lesson as a realistic target. Of these 15–20 words, perhaps only 10–12 will be retained productively, depending on the amount of practice and the amount or revisiting and recycling that takes place for the same words. A vocabulary course of 60 hours, at any level, could reasonably be expected to cover about 1000 words, though learners will certainly pick up words in other lessons on the English curriculum, as well as from reading outside of class and incidental exposure to music, films, TV and so on.

In this chapter we have looked at words, what they are, how they are formed, how many of them there are in English, what problems learners may have with their forms, how many words learners need to and can learn, and how we might begin to tackle the problem as teachers. But words also have *meanings*, and so Chapter 2 will deal with how words mean, and the implications for teaching and learning.

Chapter review

1 What do we call the underlined parts of these words?

<u>im</u>possible   <u>un</u>safe   <u>de</u>-classify

2 Which two of these words have a suffix?

makes   openness   hopeful   cooked

3 What English compounds can you make by combining words in Box A with words in Box B?

Box A	cell	snow	hill	key	shoe

Box B	top	board	lace	phone	storm

4 Only one of the following statements is true. Which one?

a. *Looks* is a derived form of the verb *look*.

b. *Looks* is an example of a blend (*look* + *s*).

c. *Looks* is an inflected form of the verb *look*.

5 How many morphemes are there in each of these words?

dog
worldwide
unthinkable
boredom

6 Fill in the blanks with the correct name for the type of word formation:

FBI, CIA, BBC, WHO are examples of _____

Brunch, blog, motel are examples of _____

Flu, gym, maths are examples of _____

7 Underline the stressed parts of these words and compounds.

ridiculous
happiness
bus stop
out-of-date

8 Write T (true) or F (false) after each of these statements.

a. All linguists agree on how many words educated adult native-speakers of English can understand.

b. Some linguists believe that educated adult native-speakers of English can understand 50 000 words or more.

c. In English, there are about 2000 words which work harder than all the rest.

d. Most words in English are rather infrequent.

9 If a learner understands 90 per cent of the words in a text, is it likely they will need any extra help or resources to understand it completely?

10 Why might the fact that English has both Anglo-Saxon words and Greek-Latin words cause problems for learners?

2 | Words and their meanings

How do words mean?

TASK 1

- Can you think of four words for this animal from four different languages? Use an online dictionary if you do not know other languages.

- Write down what you imagine when you think of this animal.

One of the most influential works in the study of words and their meanings is that of Ferdinand de Saussure. His book, *Course in General Linguistics,* based on his lectures, was published in 1916 after his death, by his former students. Key to our understanding of meaning are the following ideas based on de Saussure's work:

- Language is made up of *signs.*
- Each *sign* has two aspects:
    1. **The signifier** – the letters that make up the shape and sound of a word, for example, d-o-g /dɒg/
    2. **The signified** – the mental concept that we have in our minds when we see or hear this word, for example, *a four-legged animal, often kept as a pet ...*

In Task 1 above, you made a list of four words. Perhaps some of the following are on your list: *dog, chien, perro, hund, cão, cane, koira,* 개, 犬. Though the images that we each have in our minds may vary a little when we hear or read these words, we all agree that they signify what is represented in the picture in Task 1. This brings us to one of the core concepts of how words mean. Words are just signs. Words vary across languages and do not have intrinsic value. What makes them mean or connect to the signified is that we agree about them within our societies. As de Saussure (1974: 118) puts it, signs function not through their intrinsic value but through their relative position. What this means is:

- We agree, in English, for example, that *dog* means a four-legged animal that we often keep as a pet and that can be used for hunting and so on.

- We also agree the meaning of *dog* in relation to what it is not. For example, it does not mean a small, furry, four-legged feline animal with a tail and claws. For that, we have the word *cat*. Nor does it mean:

- When we see or hear the word *dog*, we also connect it to the concept of a dog by its shape and sound. It is not *bog, log, dig,* etc.

Most fundamentally of all, what de Saussure has shown us by making the distinction between the signifier and the signified is that the relationship between words and their meanings is arbitrary. The words we use, some for centuries, are based on chance rather than being fixed, intrinsic or based on reason.

Words can have more than one meaning (polysemy)

TASK 2

Study the two examples under each of the words: *race, wing* and *handsome*. Each example shows the word used in a different meaning.

    Race *Meaning:* close ☐ distant ☐
She ran her **race** in two hours 45 minutes.
The concept of **race** divides humans into populations or groups on the basis of various sets of characteristics.

    Wing *Meaning:* close ☐ distant ☐
The bird flapped its **wings** furiously.
We were given an office in the west **wing** of the building.

Handsome *Meaning:* close ☐ distant ☐
My grandfather was a tall **handsome** man.
They are going to make a **handsome** profit on the property.

As the examples in Task 2 show, one word can occur in different contexts and can have many meanings. We use the term **polysemy** to refer to this.

Sometimes the meaning can be close or related (as in the cases of *wing* and *handsome*) but sometimes the meaning can be distant and unrelated, as in the case of *race.* When words have the same form but different meanings, we say that they are **homonyms.**

TASK 3

The missing words are homonyms. Can you guess what each word is?

Word	Examples
	I put all my money in the _____. We sat by the river _____ and had our picnic.
	There's no hot water in the _____. I always _____ my feet in time to the music.
	We saw a _____ flying in our garden in the darkness. Many people are afraid of them. In baseball, we use a _____ with which to hit the ball.

Closeness of meaning can be as a result of some shared physical properties. For example, in the case of *the wing of the bird* and *the wing of a building*, they share the sense of being a part that sticks out. This meaning can be extended beyond the literal to the non-literal (figurative) and we can find *wing* used to describe a political group or party whose views are different or 'stick out' from the norm, *He was a member of the military wing of the ANC*. This is also the case in the examples above for *handsome*. The first example means a man who is physically attractive, whereas the second example takes this meaning and extends it in a non-literal way – that is, figuratively – to describe large profit (which is seen as attractive). This causes challenges for the teaching of vocabulary which we will discuss in Part B of this chapter.

VOCABULARY FILE

Almost all words are polysemous, except for specialist words, such as technical and scientific vocabulary, where it is often important that words have only one meaning.

Word	Definition
Ailerons	hinged control surfaces attached to the trailing edge of the wing of an aircraft.
Catheter	a medical term meaning a long thin tube used to take fluids out of the body.
Cryptosporidiosis	a intestinal disease caused by microscopic parasites.
Plectrum	a small flat tool used to pluck or strum a stringed instrument.

Often, the more frequent a word is, the more meanings it is likely to have. For example *get*:

Sentence	Definition of get
I got four birthday presents.	to receive something
I got it at a bargain price.	to buy something
Sheila got us a takeaway.	to go somewhere to bring back someone or something
Ring, ring . . . . Can you get that?	to answer the phone
I got a terrible flu last winter.	to become ill

TASK 4

Can you think of as many meanings as possible for *take*?

Meaning changes over time

Another challenge is that meaning changes over time. What a society agrees as the meaning of a given word can change. People used to go to the *pictures* and now they go to the *movies* or the *cinema*. There are many words that we now use in relation to technology that used to be associated with other meanings. Therefore, changes in society bring about changes in meanings:

Mouse

Wireless

Can you think of the old and the new meanings of these words?

	Old meaning	New meaning
menu		
notepad		
click		
spam		
site		
web		

Denotative versus connotative meaning

Denotative meaning is the core meaning of a word or phrase, the literal meaning. For example, *home* means the place where you live. *Home* also has emotional meanings associated with it and these are often subjective. *Home* can mean *a place of comfort and security, a warm and loving place with my family,* and so on. This is its **connotative meaning.** Connotative meanings may be specific to each individual and they may also be collective, within small or large groups or within cultures. Another example is the word *cow.* It denotes a four-legged animal which produces milk, but its connotation will vary across cultures. In some cultures, the cow has religious or sacred connotations.

1 Write down the denotative meaning for each of these words.
2 Write your own connotative meanings in relation to each word.
3 In each case, decide whether the connotative meaning you have described is personal or held by a group of people, culture or society.

	Denotation	Connotations	personal/societal
eagle			
heart			
feminist			
Paris			
hitchhiking			

Denotation versus sense

Words have their literal or denotative meaning but they also derive meaning in relation to other words. For example, the word *rough* has the core meaning 'an uneven surface' but it also gains its meaning from its relationship with *smooth*. *Smooth* is the opposite of *rough* but *smooth* and *rough* are bound up in each other's meaning. It is difficult to explain *rough* without reference to *smooth* and vice versa. The 'oppositeness' of *rough* and *smooth* is called a **sense relationship**. When two words have opposite meanings we say they are **antonyms**, or that they have an antonymous sense relationship. Using sense relationships can be very useful when we are explaining the meaning of new words in the classroom. In Chapter 7, we will look in detail at sense relationships between words.

When we use a particular word in speaking or writing, we choose it over another word. For example, in the statement *They have a black cat*, the colour *black* is chosen over other colours, such as *grey, white, brown,* and so on. Words such as *black, white, grey* and *brown* have meanings in the real world, but they also gain meaning in relation to each other. *Black* is the opposite or **antonym** of *white*. The cat is not *white*. *Grey* and *brown* are not antonyms of each other, nor of *black* or *white*, but they share the quality of being colours. We can say that they are **co-hyponyms**. Black, grey, white, blue, orange and red (and so on) are *hyponyms* of *colour*:

A hyponym tree for *colour*:

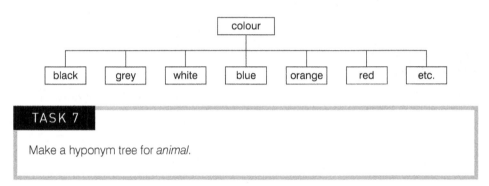

Another sense relationship between words is that of **synonymy**. This is where different words have similar meanings. Some words are very close synonyms and are often used interchangeably, for example, *couch* and *sofa*. Other synonyms may have the same meaning but, when it comes to using them, we are careful to choose the right one for the specific context. For example, the word *bicker* is synonymous with *argue* and *quarrel*. But we cannot use them interchangeably. *Bicker* means to argue usually about unimportant things whereas a *quarrel* is a bit more serious as it means an angry disagreement between people. *Argue* can mean a disagreement with someone (*We argue a lot*) but we very often use *argue* to mean 'discuss or make a point', especially when we are writing in an academic context (for example, *In this essay, I will argue that …, It is argued that …*)

Connotation and register

The connotation that a word acquires relates to feeling, emotional responses, opinions and evaluations. Like denotative meanings, the connotative meaning of a word can change over time, as well as across societies. For example, the core denotative meaning of the word *cool* used to only refer to a slightly low temperature. Now, its connotative meaning is associated with what is fashionable, trendy or attractive within popular culture; *I bought a really cool DVD*, for example. Connotations also change when we combine certain words. A word like *football* is neutral, but when you add *hooligan* to it, it takes on a very pejorative connotation.

Register is another level of meaning. It refers to how language is used in certain fields and activities relative to the roles and relationships between speakers and listeners, and readers and writers. For example, we can talk about the language of business having its own register and within that we can see how managers' and employees' use of language may vary. We can see how written business language is usually more formal than everyday written language. The language which is used at meetings is different to the language used at home around the dinner table.

Talking about a car design

Example of language used in business

The company believes that it is possible to re-engineer the model without disbanding the functional divisions and is using the development of the new model as a template for its new programs.

In everyday language

The car can be redesigned without making many changes to how we do it, and what we learn in the process will help us with designing in the future.

TASK 8

Can you identify which registers these sentences come from? Circle the words which tell you the register.

1. There was an equal distribution of radiological stage-2 and stage-3 lesions, and it seems that the mean interval between the onset of the tumour and the detection of lung metastases was 4.1 years.
2. Okay, today I want to talk to you about operating systems. An operating system controls the tasks that your computer performs in addition to managing its resources so as to optimise its performance.
3. Chop the lamb into cubes and marinade for at least an hour in the aromatic spices. Meanwhile sweat the onion and garlic and gradually add the coconut milk.
4. We usually sit here and then we'll suddenly hear Mark talking and we look over there's Brian having a laugh at all the other boys saying something to him about us girls. We just wonder what he's saying.

VOCABULARY FILE

Register is also about levels of formality. Sometimes synonyms belong to different registers:

Informal	Formal
kids	children
husband or wife	spouse
get off the train	alight
get off the plane	disembark

Understanding words under their different meanings

For learners, the effect of polysemy is that they constantly come across words which they recognise but which mean something different. As we mentioned, the most frequently used words in our lexicon usually have a number of meanings. It will help our learners to know that they always need to be on the lookout for new meanings of the words that they already know. Helping your students to guess meaning in context is also a strategy which will help them to 'attack' new words independently, so as to tease out their meaning. It is also good for learners to realise that native speakers, too, have to guess the meaning of some words which they come across. For example, most native speakers of English would have to deduce the meaning of more than one of the words in the following extract from an academic paper. The reader would use clues from the context to work out the meanings of the words that they didn't know, or they may have to use a dictionary.

> The conditions existing in each of these states are shown in Figure 2, which explicates our expansion of liminality as a heuristic for understanding and reinvigorating challenging, complex, meaningful learning.

> (Nelson and Harper, 2006: 1)

Distinguishing synonyms

The fact that some words are **synonymous**, or have the same meaning, seems like an advantage for learners but it can also cause problems. Two words are rarely completely synonymous, except perhaps words in different varieties of English, such as *kerb* (British English) and *sidewalk* (American English). There are almost always some differences, and this is a problem for language learners. We need to be careful, therefore, when teaching vocabulary through synonyms. Even the most straightforward-looking examples of synonymy involve subtle differences. For example *low* and *short*, both mean 'not high' but we cannot use *low* to describe a person's height.

She's so short.
Not: *She's so low.*

Learning new meanings as a process

Learning new meanings comes over time. It is an incremental process. Because words are polysemic, learners are faced with having to constantly learn more about the new meanings of the words they already know. It is best to look at vocabulary acquisition as a process.

It is important to constantly expose learners to new embodiments of words, so that they can gain exposure to their polysemic nature.

Within this process, students are faced not only with the challenge of increasing the breadth of their vocabulary in terms of adding new words, but they also have to simultaneously increase the depth of their knowledge about the more frequently used words in the English lexicon.

Register and connotation

Another challenge which faces learners is that some words are register-specific and some words have certain connotations. In the case of register, this relates to specific domains in which language is used, for example, the language of law, business, academia, the media, everyday conversation, and so on. In the case of connotation, it is more tricky because connotations grow and change within societies.

Acquiring a core procedural vocabulary

An important function of the core words of our lexicon, the words which are most polysemic, is their use in describing and categorising other words. Therefore, learners need to know a critical amount of core vocabulary in order to help them understand other more specialised vocabulary items. These words are sometimes referred to as '**procedural vocabulary**' (Widdowson, 1983). Many would argue that these words are more useful than specialised vocabulary because they help us to get at the specialised language through paraphrase. Let's consider some examples.

Examine the words used to describe *cutlet, chop* and *steak*. Notice the procedural words in the definitions which help to categorise and explain the meaning. If a learner knows most of these words, it will allow him/her access to the meaning of the new words *cutlet, chop* and *steak*.

cutlet – a *small piece* of *meat* still *attached* to the **bone** that can be *fried* or *grilled.*

chop – a *small piece* of *meat* *cut* with the **bone** still in it, usually from the *ribs* of a *sheep* or *pig.*

steak – a thick *flat piece* of *beef* or *fish* without *fat* on it.

L1 transfer and false friends

Some words are similar in two languages because they come from the same source, for example, *art, animal, police* and *table* are the same, or very similar, in a number of languages. We refer to these as **cognates** (see McCarthy, 1990: 50). This transfer can be both a help and a hindrance. Firstly, while some words are cognate, their meaning may not totally coincide. Secondly, a number of these cognates are 'false friends'. They look the same but they do not actually mean the same. For example, in Italian, the verb *controllare* looks like it might be a cognate of the English verb *control*, but in fact it means *check*. This can therefore lead to L1 transfer errors, such as, *We hired a security guard to control the grounds of the tennis club at night* instead of *We hired a security guard to check the grounds of the tennis club at night*.

Pre-teaching and post-teaching of meaning

Key to the teaching of meaning is the ongoing development of students' ability to draw on context to try to figure out new meanings. By engaging with contexts before a reading or listening task, students draw on their schematic knowledge. We usually have a considerable store of schematic knowledge before we read. Even as native speakers, our minds subconsciously gather together the words we know and the ideas that we have in relation to the topic of the text. Prolonging this phase in the language classroom is extremely beneficial. Starting by focusing on the topic, through a picture or a broad open-ended question, will allow learners time to retrieve the vocabulary that they already know in relation to the topic. It will also stimulate prediction about the words that are likely to be encounter. Therefore, pre-task work on vocabulary is crucially important.

If we were introducing the following text on the topic of a road accident, it would be beneficial to start with at least one of the following activities to focus on the context, on the words which the learners already know, on the ones which need to be pre-taught and the ones which can be guessed from context.

- Show the headline of the article to the students *Wrong car destroyed when firemen rescue already-rescued victims*. Ask them to think about what the story in the article might be about.
- Ask the students to predict five words that they will find in the text. Gather these on the board.
- Ask students to use their dictionaries to find three words which they don't know but which they expect to find in the article.

Wrong car destroyed when firemen rescue already-rescued victims

A Swedish taxi driver who came across an accident allowed three injured people to rest in his taxi while they waited for emergency services to arrive. The cabbie from central Sweden said: 'They had a few cuts and bruises and I let them shelter in my cab. They looked worse than they were. I went off to look at the wreck and, when the firemen turned up, they pulled out hydraulic metal cutters and sliced the side off the cab. They said it meant they could get the people out without them having to bend too much, in case of neck injuries. They didn't realise they only had to open the door.' However, a head doctor at the local hospital said that sawing off the roof to remove accident victims is the safest way to manage injuries of this kind.' The taxi driver's insurance company does not believe his story.

Teaching vocabulary directly

Some vocabulary lends itself to be taught more directly and more vividly than others, for example, action words such as *run, walk, skip, sweep, jump, wave,* and so on. Where we can use pictures, mime, demonstrations or video clips, there is not only the advantage of teaching the word in a very memorable way; it is also done in a very direct and unambiguous manner. There is obviously a limit to the number of words which can be taught in this way but, especially at lower levels, there is plenty of scope. One fun idea is to play picture bingo to teach lexical sets such as action verbs, furniture, household objects, classroom objects and types of machines. First of all, make bingo cards with six to eight different words on each card (words can repeat, just make sure that no two cards are identical). For example:

table	chairs	sofa	cupboard
television	kettle	cooker	sink

Once each student has a bingo card, the teacher uses pictures as prompts. The class call out the word when prompted by the picture and check whether it is on their card. If they have the word, they tick it off. The first to get a complete card, shouts 'bingo!'. Students usually enjoy taking turns at being the person who holds up the picture cards. Generally, the person who wins gets to do it for the next game. A variation on this is to use mime rather than pictures in the second and subsequent rounds.

How do we teach abstract words?

Teaching abstract vocabulary is more challenging. There are a number of strategies and guidelines which can help. Most of these strategies involve relating to what the students already know.

- **Draw on the world of the learner.** Relate abstract words as much as possible to the world of your learners. For example, if you are teaching the word *dreary*, ask learners to think of the nicest place where they have ever been (this activates the antonymous meaning) and then ask them to think of the least nice place that they have ever been. Link this to the new word *dreary*. Discuss what makes a place *dreary*. By associating this word with an individual place where students have been, they are more likely to remember it.

- **Break words up.** Many abstract words have prefixes and suffixes which will help decode the meaning. By developing this strategy, students will gain skills for independently working out the meaning of new words. For example, *misbehaviour* can be broken up and it is possible that students will be able to constructs its meaning in context, especially if they are familiar with the prefix *mis-*.

- *Draw on the context.* When teaching new words which are abstract in meaning, it is best to do so in context, that is, where the words are linked to the context of a story in a text. This will provide a schematic environment for the new concept. For example, it is far easier to teach a word like *loneliness* in the context of a story about someone who is living alone. In context the word has meaning which is linked to other words that the learners already know and it is part of the schema of the story. This will make it more memorable as well as more accessible.

Teaching sense relations

Try to draw on any synonyms, antonyms or hyponyms that you think your learners will already know. For example, if you were teaching the word *drench,* students will know *wet*, and being able to explain *drench* using *very wet* will link the new word to an existing word and concept. We will discuss sense relations in greater detail in Chapter 7.

Encouraging note-keeping

Encouraging your learners to keep vocabulary notebooks is very beneficial. Not only does it record the new words and their meanings, it also has the advantage of allowing students to see how many words they have learnt. This will motivate them to go on adding to their notebook. How the words are logged in the notebook is also important. It is worth working with your learners on how best to record new words and their meanings.

VOCABULARY FILE

Help your students to make links to the words that they already know and encourage them to write the meaning in English rather than in their first language.

As learners amass their new vocabulary, it is important to stress that many new words might actually be old ones with new meanings because most common words are used over and over again in their different meanings. It is a good idea to encourage students to use dictionaries to add at least one new meaning to a word which they have in their vocabulary notebook. For example:

Look up these common words in a dictionary and find two new meanings that you didn't already know.

Word	Meaning that I know	New meanings
face		
book		
train		
leave		

Reading and concordancing

Studies on vocabulary acquisition tell us of the value of learning words through several contextual encounters (Mezynski, 1983; Stahl and Fairbanks, 1986; Krashen, 1989; Nation, 1990). The more our students see, read, write, or say a word, the more likely they are to retain it in their long-term memory. Reading independently will especially help build advanced vocabulary. Reading more in English, according to Krashen (1989), facilitates multi-contextual lexical acquisition. However, Cobb (1997) argues that, in reality, few language learners have time to do enough reading for natural, multi-contextual lexical acquisition. Our students read less in general nowadays for many reasons, not least of all, the competing attractions of other media such as the Internet, television and computer games. Cobb and other supporters of **data-driven learning (DDL)** tell us that it has a lot of potential for enhancing and even accelerating vocabulary acquisition. The primary focus of DDL is at the word level, and so it allows for very focused vocabulary work. Cobb (1997) points to the potential of DDL to provide many and varied encounters with new vocabulary, or as he puts it, 'multiple contextual encounters.' In Chapters 3 and 4, we will look at how concordance lines can help in vocabulary development. Here is a basic DDL task to develop vocabulary:

TASK 9

Use an online concordancer to look up the word *hand*. What new uses of the word can you find? Add them to your vocabulary notebook.

In conclusion, we have looked at how words mean and we have seen that it is a complex matter. Words have signs but these are arbitrarily connected to their meanings because groups and societies have decided that a certain form means a certain thing. Other complexities lie in the polysemic nature of words and the fact that meaning is not static. It changes over time as new needs arise within our societies, particularly through technology. We also saw that meaning is relative to other words; meanings have relationships. Some words have the same meaning, some words have opposite meanings, and some words include other words in their meanings. We also looked at how words have connotative meanings and how their meaning can vary in different registers. All of this poses many challenges for our learners. We can help them especially by providing good note-keeping strategies and by encouraging extensive reading so that they constantly encounter words in new contexts and subtle nuances of meaning.

Chapter review

1 What is the key importance of de Saussure's distinction between *signifier* and *signified* for the teaching and learning of vocabulary?

   a. There is a one-to-one relationship between the signifier and the signified.

   b. There is an arbitrary or chance relationship between the signifier and the signified.

c. The signifier is more important than the signifier.

d. The signified is more important than the signifier.

2 Most words are polysemic. Provide two meanings with examples for each of the following words:

fringe, terribly, key, light

3 The words in bold in the sentences below have the same form but different meanings. What do we call this relationship?

a. A young cow is called a **calf.**

b. The back of the lower part of your leg is called your **calf.**

4 Only one of the following statements is true. Can you identify it?

a. The more frequent a word, the more homonyms it will have.

b. The more frequent a word, the more meanings it is likely to have (polysemic).

c. The less frequent a word, the more meanings it is likely to have (polysemic).

d. The more frequent a word, the fewer meanings it is likely to have.

5 Provide a denotative and connotative meaning for each of the following words:

Word	Denotative meaning	Connotative meaning
hippy		
dove		
beach		

6 Fill in the blanks.

_____ _____ _____ are co-hyponyms of *vehicle.*

_____ _____ _____ are co-hyponyms of *furniture.*

_____ and *cold* are antonyms.

Automobile and _____ are synonyms.

7 Give one example of a formal register and one example of an informal register.

8 In the definition of bait below, identify the procedural vocabulary:

Bait is food which you put on a hook or in a trap in order to catch fish or animals.

(Source: *Collins Cobuild Advanced Learners Dictionary of American English,* 2007, page 89)

9 What are *cognates* and what are their advantages and disadvantages for learners?

10 How can extensive reading and working with concordance lines help in vocabulary development?

3 | Collocations

What is collocation?

Which combinations of words in the table sound natural, and which sound unnatural? Mark each with **N** (natural) or **U** (unnatural), as in the example.

heavy rain	N
heavy bag	
heavy sunshine	
strong wind	
strong car	
powerful car	
blond hair	
blond jacket	

Collocation is all about how likely it is that two words will occur next to each other, or very near each another. For example, it is likely that we will find that *bright* and *light* will occur together, as will *bitterly* and *cold*. *Bright light* and *bitterly cold* are collocations. We say that the two words in each pair collocate with each other. We are not likely to find *bright coffee* or *bitterly hot*; those pairs of words do not collocate with each other. *Bright coffee* and *bitterly hot* are not impossible combinations – a poet might use them to stretch our imagination and to create unusual images – but they are very unlikely indeed in ordinary English. They are not typical English collocations. Collocation is about what the most likely combinations of words are; it is about probabilities.

We would not be surprised to see the sentence *The light was bright* or the sentence *The coffee they served was strong*. *Bright ... light* and *strong ... coffee* are typical English collocations. But the words which collocate do not have to be next to each other. The relationship of collocation remains even if the words are separated by, for example, a verb, or other phrases. Collocation, therefore, is a purely lexical (vocabulary) relationship, independent of grammar.

So, as well as looking at single words and compounds, as we did in Chapter 1, we need to look at how words attract each other and combine to form collocations. Collocations also tell us something about the meaning of words when they are used together in context (see McCarthy, 1990: 12–15; Sinclair, 1991). We need to see collocation as a type of meaning too, and add it to the meanings we considered in Chapter 2 and will look at in Chapter 7.

What types of words collocate with each other?

Any two words in the language can combine to form a collocation. However, the most frequent word in the language, the definite article *the*, is likely to collocate with tens of thousands of nouns; so many, in fact, that the information is not very useful for the study of vocabulary. For this reason, the definite article, and all the other most frequent words such as pronouns, prepositions, auxiliary and modal verbs and so on, are usually dealt with under the heading of grammar. They belong to the grammar class rather than the vocabulary class.

What we need to know is whether words are occurring together simply by chance or because of the way the grammar works, or whether two words are occurring with statistical significance, in other words, more than just by chance. Collocations have become established over a long period of time; they do not just happen by chance.

The less frequent a word is – if it regularly combines with another particular word – the more likely it is that this is significant and not just happening by chance. It is these combinations which are important, because they carry particular meanings that have become fixed in the language. What is more, they are difficult to predict, or to guess from intuition, and this is true for native speakers and non-native users alike. Because of this, the best way to get at the collocations of a language is to use a corpus, and let the computer do the statistical work. Biber et al. (1998: 265–8), provide a useful outline of computer methods for analysing collocations.

Since we do not usually include grammar words in the study of collocations, the typical combinations will involve the major word-classes of nouns: verbs, adjectives and adverbs.

Here are some nouns, adjectives and verbs, and a selection of their significant collocations. The information comes from a sample of 50 million words of texts from British magazines in the Bank of English corpus. The computer has calculated which words are most likely to occur significantly with the key words.

adjectives used with role	adverbs used with disappointed	nouns used as the object of create
important	bitterly	jobs
major	deeply	atmosphere
active	obviously	effect
crucial	extremely	image
central	terribly	problems

Collocations and word frequency

> **TASK 2**
>
> Underline every word which typically collocates with the key word in each line, as in the example. If the combination sounds odd or unusual, do not underline it.
>
> *key word*
> **very**   <u>noisy</u>   nice   good   dead   easy   happy   cold
> **utterly**   wrong   stupid   hard   ridiculous   hungry   old   crazy

Generally speaking, the more common a word is the more words it will collocate with. The less common a word is, the more its collocations are limited or restricted. So, very common, everyday adverbs such as *very* and *really*, which are used to strengthen or intensify an idea, will collocate with hundreds of adjectives. They will collocate more freely than adverbs with a similar intensifying function such as *utterly* or *profoundly*.

The following adjectives all occur after *very* and *really* in the Bank of English corpus, but not after *utterly* or *profoundly*:

very/really ...	
hard	high
strong	low
small	young
large	careful

We do not say *profoundly strong* or *profoundly low*, and we do not say *utterly small* or *utterly young*.

The following adjectives occur after *utterly* and *profoundly* in the Bank of English corpus. They could equally well come after *very* or *really*.

utterly	**profoundly**
different	different
reliable	disturbing
dependent	important
confused	gifted

Weak and strong collocations

Words which combine with only a small number of other words are called strong collocators. Words that will make a large number of collocations are called weak collocators. Words like *very* or *really* can form hundreds of collocations, (*very good, really difficult* and so on), but they are weak collocations. Words like *superficially* and *benignly* are far rarer; they enter into far fewer combinations and form strong collocations. Strong collocations such as *profoundly disturbing, superficially similar, benignly disposed* and *utterly reliable* are more difficult to guess or predict. Some collocations are very restricted – a particular word may collocate with only a very small number of other words. Moon (1987), for example, shows that 99 per cent of occurrences of the word *torrential* in the Bank of English corpus collocate with *rain*, with only a tiny number of other collocations occurring that are also connected with rain (*storm, downpour*).

Because there are so many collocations in the language and because they are often difficult to predict, lexicographers (people who write dictionaries) have produced special dictionaries of collocations, especially for learners. One notable example for learners of English contains 150 000 collocations based on the 100-million-word British National Corpus (OUP, 2006). Another special dictionary of collocations focuses on 2000 essential nouns and gives a total of 50 000 collocations for the nouns, as well as dealing with the other word classes (LTP, 1997). Other, general dictionaries have special ways of showing collocations. Some choose example sentences so that they include the most common collocations for the word in question. Others have special typefaces and ways of showing collocating words. COBUILD (2009) has a feature called *Word Partnerships*, where the dictionary entry gives not only the most common collocations for a headword, but also a number showing which meaning of the headword in the main entry for the word that the collocation is used with.

The *COBUILD Online* website allows you to type in a word and get a list of the most frequent collocations for that word. For example, if you type in the word *explanation*, you will immediately get a list which includes the following ten items (the common grammar words such as *an, of* and *the* have been excluded here, as discussed above):

given	plausible
simple	likely
possible	logical
offered	rational
only	satisfactory

From this list we can extract such common verb + noun collocations as *to give/offer an explanation* and adjective + noun combinations such as *a simple/possible/plausible explanation*.

Native speakers and expert users of English know thousands of collocations and usually have a good sense of how weak or how strong a word is in terms of its ability to combine with other words. Bolinger (1976), Pawley and Sider (1983), Peters (1983) and Sinclair (1991) are among linguists who argue that native speakers know more than just single words – they also know how the words combine into collocations and longer phrases and chunks (see Chapter 5), and have thousands of these stored in memory. Native speakers and expert users also know what the collocations mean as a unit, as well as the meaning of the individual words that make them up.

Collocations and meanings

TASK 3

Explain briefly the different meanings of the verbs in bold, depending on the words they collocate with:

go home	**go** crazy
get a new computer	**get** the phone
make dinner	**make** a noise
catch a bus	**catch** a cold

Some of the most frequent verbs in English have many different meanings. The dozens of different meanings for verbs like *get, do,* and *make* can cover page after page in a dictionary. For *get, do* and *make*, and for other similar verbs such as *go, come* and *take*, their meanings are often best understood by looking at the words they collocate with.

We can learn a lot about what words mean by looking at the collocations they enter into. Often, several words may appear to mean the same or to have very similar meanings – they are **synonyms,** or near-synonyms (see Chapters 2 and 7). In such cases, it is often how the words collocate with other words that can show up differences. Let us consider, for example, *strong* and *powerful*. Sometimes they can be used with very similar meanings:

strong/powerful leader   strong/powerful voice
strong/powerful argument   strong/powerful (wo)man
strong/powerful presence   strong/powerful ocean current

However, in the 50-million-word sample of the Bank of English corpus, which is made up of British magazines, some collocations only occur with one of the words:

Collocations with *strong* but not *powerful*: *strong coffee, strong marriage, strong views*
Collocations with *powerful* but not *strong*: *powerful car, powerful computer, powerful engine*

We can also see how different senses of the same word collocate differently when we look at the collocations of their opposites in meaning (their **antonyms –** see Chapters 2 and 7). Here are some examples:

collocation	opposite
dark hair	fair hair
dark colours	light colours
light winds	strong winds
light rain	heavy rain
happy song	sad song
happy marriage	unhappy marriage

Collocations and register

In Chapter 2, we discussed connotation and register. Here we will show how technical and specialist registers such as legal English, computer English, academic English or business English have developed their own sets of collocations which contribute to the character of the registers, providing a sort of 'fingerprint' of the special type of language.

Changes in society, in technology and human activity in general – in addition to producing new words and new compounds – also produce new collocations. Collocations change over time, just as single words do. Computers have brought a number of new collocations into our daily lives, such as these verb + noun ones:

surf the Web   *burn a CD*
download a document   *clone an image*
insert a hyperlink   *paste a selection*
create an identity   *unzip a file*

Thirty years ago, almost no-one would have understood what these collocations meant. New collocations often create shifts in meaning for the individual words: surfing the Web has nothing to do with beaches or the sea and does not involve a surfboard, and burning a CD does not mean setting fire to it!

Dictionaries of special register collocations have been created using corpora, just as general dictionaries of collocations have. Longman (2007), for example, contains many thousands of typical business English collocations, indicated in bold typeface within the headword entries.

Collocation is a powerful organising principle in the vocabulary of English, both in general English and in special registers. It is not enough just to know the thousands of words we discussed in Chapter 1. We also have to know how they go together, and this is a problem for anyone learning English as a second or foreign language. Often, collocation is not really a question of right and wrong. Many word combinations will not be 'wrong', but they may be unusual, unnatural and very unlikely. There are no 'rules' about collocation in the way that there are grammatical rules such as how to form the present tense of verbs. This creates particular problems, both for the learner and for teachers and materials writers.

How well do learners learn and use collocations?

TASK 5

Think of when you were learning English in school or at college or university. Did your teachers or course books ever mention collocation? If not, did you learn collocations indirectly, or by another name (such as word pairs or word combinations)?

One obvious answer to the question posed in the title of this section is that it depends on the language level of the learners, the extent to which they are exposed to collocations, how aware they are of them, how much practice they are given in using them, and so on. This will vary greatly in syllabuses and classrooms around the world and in different course books and other materials that students use. However, there seems to be a general consensus among researchers that learners of English, even those with higher levels of proficiency, have problems with English collocations. They either use collocations which are not typical, or they simply translate collocations from their first language, or else they under-use or over-use certain types of collocations.

VOCABULARY FILE

If learners use collocations that are not typical, a possible explanation is that they are translating from their first language (L1).

A Spanish-speaking learner of English might say 'make a question' instead of 'ask a question' because the verb in the Spanish collocation *hacer una pregunta* corresponds to the English verb *make* rather than *ask*. Farghal and Obiedar (1995) suggest that learners often do indeed over-rely on translation from L1. Another possible explanation is that learners are creating phrases and sentences word-by-word, choosing correct words but not thinking of whether the words collocate or not. That is to say, learners create language **bottom-up**. Native speakers and expert users, because they have stored thousands of ready-made collocations, are working **top-down**, and simply accessing collocations from memory. This problem may be especially apparent among beginning learners, where the cognitive pressures of creating sentences in a strange new language mean that words are accessed one by one. But one reason for bottom-up production may also be the way learners are taught; if the vocabulary lesson is always focusing on single words, and if language is taught with an over-emphasis on grammar, students may see production as question of filling empty grammatical slots (such as subject, auxiliary + main verb, object, adverb + adjective and so on) with single words.

Another way in which learners might use non-typical collocations is by over-using some collocations at the expense of others. So, for example, learners who know the adjective *big* might be tempted to use it in collocations where English would prefer *large* or *great*. In an 80-million-word sample of British news texts in the Bank of English corpus, some of the collocations of *great* can also occur with *big* (such as *great/big success, great/big contribution*), but many simply do not. So, we do not find *big distance, big amount* or *big respect*, even though those nouns collocate with *great*. There is some evidence that learners do, in fact, over-use collocations in this way; O'Dell and McCarthy (2008), for example, identify untypical collocations such as *very delighted* (instead of *really/absolutely delighted*) and *a little decrease* (instead of *a slight decrease*), based on learner corpus evidence.

But learners may also under-use typical collocations in comparison with how native speakers use them. Howarth, for example, looked at verb + noun collocations in native-speaker and learner corpora and concluded that 'native speakers employ about 50 per cent more restricted collocations and idioms than learners do' (1998: 177). Granger (1998: 152) also concluded that learners under-use native-like collocations in combinations such as intensifying adverbs used with adjectives. The adverbs *completely* and *totally* were more frequent in the learner data than in the native speaker data. On the other hand, *highly* was used more often by the native speakers than by the learners, possibly due to translation from the learners' L1 (French). Granger also concluded that learners' general awareness of collocations was poor.

Learning special registers

The task of learning the language of special registers is a daunting one, but often learners who are aiming to become proficient in, say, academic English or business English already have a fairly large vocabulary from their profession or subject area. The collocations in their particular area may have slightly different meanings to what the same collocations mean in general English. So the collocation *going forward*, in general English, tends to mean either moving forward in space (for example, a vehicle can go forward), or making progress in some activity. However, in the 80-million-word sample of British news texts in the Bank of English corpus, in business-related texts, we often find the collocation *going forward* meaning 'from this point in time into the future', in sentences such as: *We can look forward to continued growth, going forward*. One might argue that collocations are at least as important in learning the special or technical language of a particular profession or activity as the individual words, or even more important. This is because, although individual words are often shared across subjects and disciplines, collocations involving those words may not be shared across different subjects (Ward, 2007).

A final problem concerning special registers is that learners might create untypical collocations based on their knowledge of single words within a register, thinking they will be safe in doing so because both words belong to the register. Taiwo (2004) gives examples such as *borrow a loan* (instead of *take out a loan*) and *type the keyboard* (instead of *use the keyboard*). These untypical collocations are understandable, given the relationship between the single words that make them up.

Most researchers who have looked at learners' problems with collocation agree that the best way to tackle the problems is to help learners become aware of collocations and how they work in the language. Without awareness, it would be very puzzling for learners to have to work with collocation exercises and activities. Very few learners will come to class expecting to learn collocations; for most learners their expectations are that the teachers and course books will teach them grammar, vocabulary (probably in the form of hundreds of single words), pronunciation and perhaps skills such as writing or speaking. So, the teacher's or textbook's first responsibility is to create awareness of what collocation is and how it can improve the learner's English.

There are two basic ways of raising awareness: direct and indirect, and teachers will know best which one is more suitable for their students. The direct way means actually using the term 'collocation' in the classroom, explaining what it means and giving examples, then going on to various activities and exercises. This is a **deductive** way of teaching collocation: the teacher explains the principle, next the students apply it and work with examples, then they find more examples, and so on. This follows the principle of 'noticing' – if students can notice and find more examples for themselves, they have more chance of acquiring new language. For more on this, the *Teaching English* website produced by the British Council and the BBC has some useful articles on working with collocations. There is no reason to think that the word *collocation* is any more difficult for students to understand than a word like *noun* or *subject* or *intonation*. Once students are familiar with the term, collocation can become a regular and familiar feature of the vocabulary lesson. However, teachers may decide that introducing the idea of collocation by the direct method will be more suitable for higher-level learners. Every teacher knows their own learners best.

The other way of introducing collocation, the indirect way, lends itself more to an **inductive** approach. The idea here is that learners practice putting words into pairs through various simple activities, after which the teacher can explain what was behind the activities. In this way, the general principle of collocation comes out of the individual examples and activities, the opposite of the direct, deductive approach. An example of the indirect way would be to give out two sets of cards to the class. On one set could be verbs, on the other set, nouns. The task is for each student with a verb card to find a student with a noun card which can follow that verb. For example, verb cards might contain words like *catch, make, take*, while the noun cards contain words like *dinner, a break, a bus*. Putting the right cards together will give combinations such as *make dinner, take a break, catch a bus* and so on. The teacher can then talk about how important it is to get the right combinations of words, and they may or may not call these 'collocations'; they may prefer to call them 'word pairs', or 'word partners', or something that might be easier for learners to understand. The main point is to raise awareness. With easy words like those in the example above, using the indirect method, the general principle of collocation can therefore be introduced at quite low levels, from elementary onwards.

Once the principle of collocation is established, different kinds of exercises and activities can then be used to practice and consolidate it. Gap-fill exercises can be used where one word of the pair is missing; these can be done as cloze tests in short texts or simply as lists of word-pairs where one word of the pair is missing. Word-forks are also a good way of practising the most common collocations of a word. For example:

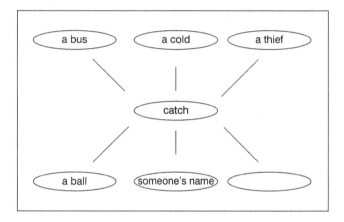

Which items from the list can you put into the word-fork?

an effort   *a mistake*   *your homework*   *a meal*   *your duty*

make —| *an effort*
      |_____
      |_____

Bubble-diagrams are also a good visual way of recording collocations; they appeal to learners who prefer a more visual approach to learning things:

a bus   a cold   a thief

catch

a ball   someone's name

Students can fill empty bubbles, use a dictionary to find more collocations and add more bubbles, and so on.

VOCABULARY FILE

Using a dictionary in conjunction with classroom activities is important, because, although good learners' dictionaries give useful information about collocations, students often under-use their dictionaries and are not aware of the dictionary as a resource for information over and above meaning and spelling (Béjoint, 1981). Once they become aware, they are likely to use their dictionaries more efficiently.

Collocation quizzes can also be both fun and useful, especially if they can be done electronically, online or on CD-ROM, where students can get instant feedback and a score which they can try to improve over time. Several websites offer online collocation quizzes; just do a search for 'collocation quiz' in your Web browser.

Published materials focusing on collocations (usually at intermediate and advanced levels) include a variety of quizzes, games, puzzles, gap-fill exercises, re-write exercises, visual activities, and so on, which present and practise collocations in familiar, non-threatening ways to students (for example, McCarthy and O'Dell, 2005; Marks and Wooder, 2007). These materials often emphasise that learning and using collocations will improve the learner's style in writing, and make their English more natural.

Probably the most important aspect of learning collocations is recording them in a vocabulary notebook as, otherwise, they will be difficult to remember. Students very often record only single words and their L1 translations in their notebooks, so they may need training here too (see Schmitt and Schmitt, 1995). McCarthy et al. (2005–2006) stress the importance of the vocabulary notebook and have notebooks, which students can use and expand, in-built in both the books and accompanying CD-ROMs of their four-level adult English course, and which include practise in recording collocations.

Since vocabulary learning is such a huge task, and since there seem to be so many individual words and word-combinations, anything we can do to organise the learning process will almost certainly lead to better and more long-lasting learning. Getting collocation information from a corpus is the first step towards this kind of organisation. Choosing collocations according to the word-classes which commonly combine with each other (adjective + noun, verb + adverb, for example) is a very useful way of organising collocations for teaching and learning, and most good materials and activities organise vocabulary according to word-class. Strong collocations such as *profoundly disturbing* and *utterly reliable* are more difficult to guess or predict. We can therefore grade collocations, leaving the stronger ones to the more advanced levels. And exercises and activities focusing on, for example, near-synonyms, may be particularly helpful for higher-level learners who need to be able to distinguish among similar words in the large vocabularies they have already acquired (see McCarthy and O'Dell, 2008). Collocation need not be a difficult and off-putting aspect of vocabulary teaching, and, as we have shown here, can be approached at all levels, from elementary to advanced.

Chapter review

1 Which definition of collocation is correct?

a. Collocation is a relationship between words based on their word-class.

b. Collocation is a relationship between words based on a system of rules for combining words.

c. Collocation is a relationship between words based on how likely it is that two words will occur together.

d. Collocation is a relationship between words based on how close two words are to each other in a text.

2 Which of these collocations are typical (write **T**) and which are untypical (write **U**) in English?

brown hair _____

a delicious house _____

to ride a car _____

beige hair _____

a delightful house _____

to ride a horse _____

3 Which collocation is a strong collocation, which is a weak one and which is a restricted one?

very good _____ auburn hair _____ utterly ridiculous _____

4 Only one of the following statements is true. Which one?

a. Words which are synonyms enter into exactly the same collocations.

b. Words which are synonyms do not have collocations in common.

c. Words which are synonyms may have some collocations in common, and some which are different.

5 Write the opposite of the words in bold.

collocation	opposite
I prefer **dark** colours	I prefer _____ colours
She has **dark** hair	She has _____ hair
I hate **strong** coffee	I hate _____ coffee
There was a **strong** smell of petrol	There was a _____ smell of petrol

6 Which statements are true? Write **T** (true) or **F** (false).

a. There are no special dictionaries just dedicated to collocation. _____

b. An educated native speaker of English probably knows thousands of collocations. _____

c. New collocations often show a shift in the meaning of the words which combine. _____

d. Computers can't find collocations in a corpus. _____

7 What problem connected with collocation do you think this learner has? She is writing about her first time in London. How could she improve her text?

"When I arrived I was very surprised to see that the streets were very crowded. It was very difficult to walk along Oxford Street because everyone was rushing and seemed very busy. I was very confused by the London Underground trains. The city is very exciting, but I was very nervous all the time."

8 Read (A) and (B) below and decide which is an example of a deductive approach to teaching collocation and which is an example of an inductive approach.

A: The teacher explains how words combine to form collocations and gives one or two examples. He then asks the students to find examples of collocations in a text. The students then do a collocation gap-fill exercise. _____

B: In a class of 12 students, the teacher gives out cards, six with adjectives on, and six with nouns. Each student with an adjective card has to find a student with a noun card that fits the adjective. The class then discuss why the exercise is important. _____

9 How can the teacher use visual aids to teach collocation?

10 What rules can a teacher teach their students about collocation?

4 | The grammar of words

Words have grammatical relationships with other words

TASK 1

Guess the missing words in the sentence below.

Grace sat alone drinking _____ cup _____ tea _____ a chipped mug.

The sentence should read *Grace sat alone drinking a cup of tea from a chipped mug.* How did you work out the missing words? For the first missing word, you may have looked at *drinking* and *cup* and figured that an article must be needed. For the next missing word, *of*, you may have linked *cup* with *tea* to come up with the phrase *cup of tea.* In the case of the third missing word, you may have deduced from the context that the preposition *from* was needed.

Essentially, the knowledge that you drew on for this task is related to grammar as much as vocabulary. Knowing the words *drink* and *cup* alone would not have guaranteed that you could have filled the blanks successfully. You were able to draw on a store of grammatical patterns relating to *drink* and *cup.* In order to complete the task successfully, you had to know the patterns:

a cup of [tea/coffee, cocoa, and so on]
drink [something] *from a* [cup/mug/glass, and so on]

The focus of this chapter will be the grammatical relationships that words have with other words. Some of these relationships are very strong and some are more open. Essentially, words have grammatical patterns in which they are used and other patterns in which they are not used. As our vocabulary grows, so does our knowledge of typical patterns. We know that the patterns below are not correct:

---

a cup [tea/coffee, cocoa, and so on]
drink [something] to a [cup/mug/glass, and so on]

In Chapter 2, we looked at how words are related to each other through meaning or sense (see also Chapter 7). For example, *soft, soggy, mushy, feathery, flaccid* are all related to each other by their meaning 'soft'. In Chapter 3, we looked at collocation, how words are related to other words around them and how they go together with certain words and not with others, for example *a thick book* but not *a fat book, a slim person* but not *a slim sandwich*. Here, we look at how words relate to each other in grammatical patterns, that is, the grammar of words. It might seem curious that we are covering grammatical patterns in a book about vocabulary, but these patterns are an essential part of vocabulary learning.

TASK 2

Drawing on your knowledge of the grammar of words, decide which of the following patterns for the word *opinion* are correct and which are incorrect?

on my opinion
in my opinion
of my opinion
to my opinion
to be of the opinion that

If you are familiar with the word *opinion,* this task if very simple. On the other hand, if *opinion* is a new or relatively new word for you, then this task will be very challenging. In addition, you may be very familiar with the word *opinion* but it may be that in your first language all of these patterns are be possible. Knowing the correct pattern in which a word is used adds another level to vocabulary learning. Not only do we need to learn to recognise and reproduce new words, plus the words which are likely to occur with them (collocations) – such as *public* and *polls* in the case of *opinion* – we also have to learn about the grammar of the new word. *In my opinion* and *to be of the opinion that* are typical patterns of *opinion* but *on my opinion, of my opinion* and *to my opinion* are not.

Collocation and colligation

Collocation, as we know, is about how likely two words are to occur next to each other, or very near each another; it is about lexical patterns. Here, we look at how words go together in grammatical rather than lexical patterns. We call this **colligation.**

Use an online concordancer or a dictionary to find out:

1 What words collocate with *phone*?
2 What words colligate with *phone*? (That is, what grammatical patterns go with the word 'phone'?)

You may have found a number of collocates for the word *phone* such as *rang, lines, jammed, mobile, emergency, charger, calls, talk/talking, satellite, chat*. There are a number of colligational patterns for *phone*:

noun phrase + participle	*the phone rang; phone-lines jammed*
verb + prepositional phrase	*chat/speak/talk on the phone* *screaming/yelling into the phone*
verb + to + pro(noun) + prepositional phrase	*spoke/chat to Renata on the phone*
make + phone call (+ prepositional phrase)	*make a phone call to Jason* *make phone calls*
verb + particle + phone	*turn on the phone*
verb + phone + particle	*turn the phone on*

Notice the colligational patterns with the different verbs for speaking on the phone. When we say *chat, speak* or *talk*, the most common pattern is *on the phone* but when we *yell* or *scream*, we use a different grammatical pattern, we *scream* or *yell into the phone*. Colligation is therefore a relationship of syntax, whereas collocation is a relationship of words or lexis. Words collocate with certain other words but they colligate with certain grammatical patterns. Here are some more examples of how a change in the choice of word means a change in the colligational pattern:

In the sentences below, *expel, release, discharge* and *check out* share the meaning of leaving a place. Therefore, we can say that they have a sense relationship (of synonyms); you may remember sense relationships from Chapter 2. Each word has strong lexical relationships with other words (collocates): *expel + school, release + prison, discharge + hospital* and *check out + hotel*.

He was expelled from school.
He was released from prison.
He was discharged from hospital.
He checked out of the hotel.

In terms of colligation, the first three patterns are the same:

To be [-ed form of verb] from [noun].

These three patterns are in passive voice. However by choosing the word *check out* we have to use a different pattern. It would be incorrect to follow the previous pattern:

*He was checked out from hotel.

Check out differs in its colligational pattern from the other three verbs in three ways:

1 It uses active rather than passive voice.
2 It uses a different prepositional pattern (*of* rather than *from*).
3 The noun phrase includes an article, unlike *school, prison* or *hospital*.

Paradigmatic and syntagmatic relationships

Bringing what we know from Chapters 2 and 3 together with the notion of the grammar of words, we can say that words relate to each other in two ways: **paradigmatically** and **syntagmatically.** From the previous example of *expel, release, discharge* and *check out*, we can show their paradigmatic and syntagmatic relationships as follows:

Paradigmatic relationship

A paradigm is a very clear and simple example or model of something. We can say that *expel, release, discharge*, and *check out* are related to each other paradigmatically by the meaning they share of 'leaving somewhere'. This connection brings these four words together through a meaning paradigm, or a paradigmatic relationship.

Syntagmatic relationship

When we look at *expel, release, discharge*, and *check out* in terms of relationships with other words, both lexical (collocation) and grammatical (colligation), we can say that they have collocational and colligational patterns. Collocation and colligation are not about meaning relationships. Their patterns are about relationships with other words that occur next to or near *expel, release, discharge* and *check out*, and we call these syntagmatic relationships.

We can represent the paradigmatic relationship vertically and the syntagmatic relationship horizontally:

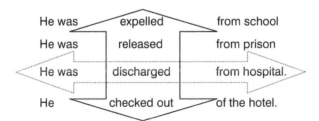

In summary, knowing about the paradigmatic and syntagmatic relationships that words have with other words is an important part of vocabulary acquisition and language competence.

Do I need a dictionary or a grammar book?

More and more, the traditional split between vocabulary and grammar is breaking down. Books on language, as well as materials for teaching, used to treat vocabulary and grammar as separate entities. Dictionaries used to deal only with words and their meanings, and grammars used to deal only with grammatical structure. A big agent of change has been the use of corpora to study language and the development of sophisticated learners' dictionaries. As a result of corpora, in addition to extensive information about meaning (paradigmatic), modern dictionaries now provide grammatical information, especially about typical patterns of a word (syntagmatic).

John Sinclair, who oversaw the COBUILD Project, is the person who has been most influential in bridging the traditional gap between lexis and grammar. He describes the process of building the 1987 COBUILD dictionary by saying that 'there was in practice no clear distinction between grammar and lexis, and grammatical rules merged with restrictions in particular instances, and those restrictions ranged from the obviously grammatical to the obviously lexical' (1987: 110). In a memorable quote from Sinclair (1991: 65) in relation to the writing of grammar books, he predicted that, 'the traditional domain of syntax will be invaded by lexical hordes'.

Modern corpus-based grammars provide a lot of information about word meaning and collocation as well as grammar (see Biber et al., 1999; Carter and McCarthy, 2006). For instance, in their 2006 grammar, Carter and McCarthy include almost 80 lexical entries. In justifying their selection, they say that these words have been included because they are very frequent in everyday language; they are often polysemous (have more than one meaning); they are individual in some way in their grammar, possessing characteristics that are worthy of particular note and/ or they are known to be difficult for learners of English and often lead to errors (2006: 17).

What patterns do we know about?

Through the use of corpora, many researchers have been able to look in detail at typical patterns of English. Hunston and Francis, for example, provide many typical patterns for nouns, verbs and adjectives. For verbs alone, the number of possible patterns spans several pages. Some examples include (2000: 53ff):

Verb + noun *I broke my arm*	**verb + reflexive pronoun** *He dressed himself*	**verb + adjective** *They left happy*
Verb + -ing *I started running*	**verb + to infinitive** *The car began to stop*	**verb + bare infinitive** *He helped paint the house.*
Verb + (pro)noun + wh- *She showed me where I should go*	**verb + wh- + to infinitive** *I'll show you how to do it.*	
Verb + noun + past participle *I had teeth extracted*	**verb + noun + preposition/ adjective** *Andrew chained the boat to the bridge* *Stir the sugar in.*	

Römer (2005) conducts a large-scale study of progressive patterns (*I was walking*) in English. She looks at more than 10 000 real examples from a corpus and compares their patterns with those which are presented in textbooks. She highlights a number of differences between the patterns which are actually used ones, and those which are presented in the textbooks.

By looking at a corpus, we can find out a lot about patterns. For example, a corpus can tell us about which prepositions follow certain verbs, which phrasal verbs can be used with a direct object and so on. In their corpus-based grammar, Carter and McCarthy (2006) list the most common particles that we use and the verbs they usually combine with. Some examples from their list are (2006: 431):

go/hang/knock/mess **about**
forge/go/keep/move **ahead**
come/go/get/take **off**
break/come/go/put **out**

Patterns and register

Register, as we've already seen, refers to how language is used in certain domains – such as business, law, academic, everyday conversation – relative to the roles and relationships between speakers and listeners and readers and writers (for example, two friends talking, a job applicant writing to a company manager, a boss talking to an employee). How we use language varies according to register, even a simple invitation to lunch might vary considerably in everyday conversation, between friends, (*Lunch?*), to a very formal written context (*We would like to cordially invite you to join us for lunch …*). A corpus is very useful for looking at different registers of language. We can divide up real samples of language into different registers – literary texts, business documents and academic papers, for example – and compare how words are used. The grammar of words can differ across registers.

TASK 4

Below are some concordance lines for the word *catch* from corpora of different registers, casual conversation and academic lectures and seminars. Compare these samples and try to identify the different patterns in each register.

(Continued)

Samples of the word *catch* from the Limerick Corpus of Irish English (LCIE, see Farr et al., 2002)

Well Deirdre tell us anyway did Terry	**catch**	any fish on Saturday evening?
they were just too much. Did you	**catch**	anything that was being said at this
and one diet coke, cos we were playing "	**catch**	-up" like. She gives your man twenty
ey were always after him but they couldn't	**catch**	him. They couldn't **catch** him doing
be rising him there every day and I does	**catch**	him out. He gets right tough with me
now. Here yeah here here.	**catch.**	mitates the sound of a throw
	catch	it by the two legs like you **catch** a
He's from Newfoudland but he's quick to	**catch**	onto our ways. What's the legal age in
aughing Sorry I didn't quite	**catch**	that? Tony is the match on
d the second thing is you'd almost want to	**catch**	them by the hand+ Umhum.

Samples of the word *catch* from the Limerick-Belfast Corpus of Academic Spoken English (LIBEL, see Walsh and O'Keeffe, 2007).

you don't have to pay anything but the	**catch**	is we're actually going to retain the
Okay sorry. Okay? I'll give you a second to	**catch**	it. Student: Miss Moore?
else does he tell us about there? Could you	**catch**	it? What a man that would
We're not saying like if your integrate you	**catch**	that bit. There's an awful lot of
<tape playing> . Did you	**catch**	that? Ah did you get that one?
t do we do? What do we tell them? You know	**catch**	up learn cop on. If Travellers are
or that one. Come on group B you've got to	**catch**	up now. So group B am number four have
n essence of I suppose a marking of another	**catch**	up phase where Ireland is coming more
eek but arrest happens at a point where they	**catch**	you. Ok all right so that's that one.

PART B What are the problems for learners?

Another layer of learning

The importance of knowing the grammar of a new word is undoubtedly crucial to language competence but this also puts extra demands on our learners. Not only do they need to know paradigmatic information on the meaning of a new word, they also need to know syntagmatic information about its collocates and its grammar (or colligates). Above all, they need to know core grammatical information about new words such as word-class and for nouns, whether they are countable or uncountable, for verbs whether they are transitive or intransitive, for adjectives and adverbs whether they are gradable (i.e. whether they can be used with words like *very*), and so on. This is a big demand but, the more comprehensively new words are introduced, then the better long-term effect on competence. For example, for a new word such as the noun *grudge*, a learner needs to know:

Word class:	noun (countable)
Meaning:	strong feelings of dislike towards someone which usually last a long time because of something they did
Collocates:	bear, have, hold, harbour (+ *a grudge*)
Colligates:	*verb + a grudge + against* someone; *bear/have a grudge + towards* someone

The learner who has attended to all of these aspects of a word will know that the following sentence is not possible:

* *She held a grudge to her parents for many years.*

VOCABULARY FILE

However, it may be unreasonable to expect that a learner will be able to learn all of these aspects to the new word when it is first encountered. If a learning strategy is in place to focus students on these aspects of a word, then the new collocates and colligations will be easier to assimilate over time, as the word is encountered in new contexts.

Negative transfer from first language

We have to recognise the immense challenge for learners when faced with choosing the correct grammatical pattern of a word because, very often, they have differing patterns in their first language. There are many typical errors that relate to colligational patterns which come from a learner's first language. Here are some examples:

* *It depends of / from my mother.* (correct pattern: *It depends on ...*)
* *'Friends' is the most popular programme in television.* (correct pattern: *... on television*)
* *Every summer we go in Italy.* (correct pattern: *... go to Italy*)
* *I'm very interesting in science.* (correct pattern: *... interested in ...*)
* *For me cycling is a funny thing to do. I love it.* (correct pattern: *... a fun thing to do ...*)

PART C How do we teach it?

At what stage?

Hoey (1991) stresses the advantages of teaching patterns from Beginners' level. He says that, even at Beginners' level, learners can identify patterns to a certain degree.

The fact that learners know colligational patterns in their first language supports this (though it can also pose quite a hindrance, as discussed above). On the other hand, we cannot expect to overload beginners with a daunting amount of information. The important things to do, even at Beginner's level, are:

- Strategically focus on patterns as new words arise.
- Develop a sense of noticing in your students.
- Compare patterns that they know from their first language and identify ones that are the same and ones that are different.
- Use vocabulary notebooks and develop strategies for note-taking.

VOCABULARY FILE

Willis (2006: 12) proposes three key learning processes for patterns. These can be applied to any level:

1 Recognition

Recognising the general phenomenon

Recognising individual phrases and patterns

2 System building

Organising phrases and patterns to make them learnable

3 Extension and exploration

Encouraging learners to extend their knowledge and enabling them to be independent

Materials to use

Another challenge for teachers and learners is that many coursebooks still hold to the traditional division between vocabulary and grammar. This means that the teacher has to try to promote systematic exploration of new words so as to attend to both paradigmatic and syntagmatic aspects. Having a good dictionary helps a lot. All of the main publishers produce corpus-based dictionaries and word entries provide information about collocation and colligation as well as meaning.

One of the most basic ways of focusing on the grammar patterns of words is through gap-filling and cloze test activities. We use these with our learners at all levels and they are a standard feature in testing and assessment. Gap-fill and cloze tests ultimately test learners' syntagmatic knowledge (collocation and colligation) and they are very worthwhile aids to vocabulary development. There are a number of Computer Assisted Language Learning (CALL) software packages that allow you to load in texts and generate your own gap-filling tasks either on paper or on a PC. One example is *Gapmaster* (published by Wida). This allows you load a text and it then creates the gaps for your task. As your students fill the blanks, the software will tell them whether it is correct or not and it keeps a running score. The software also allows for adding picture prompts and sound hints.

Storyboard (also published by Wida) is another CALL package that is very useful for building up syntagmatic knowledge. The teacher loads in a text and the learners have to reconstruct it, starting with a blank screen. When a word is entered, all of its instances will appear (if it is used in the text). Learners learn to start with the high grammatical frequency words such as articles, prepositions, auxiliary verbs and so on. The learner will usually have some context to work with and they become very motivated in trying to reconstruct all of the text. The teacher can modify the level of difficulty by providing some words or hints on screen. This activity draws heavily on learners' syntagmatic knowledge.

Using **concordances** with your students is also an excellent way of building up their knowledge of collocation and colligation. We have used concordances in this chapter to show patterns. In class, similar activities can be used but they can be carefully tailored to the level of the students. For example, why not use texts that the students are using in class as your corpus (remember to clear copyright permission before using any third party material), or perhaps use their own written work. By building up a corpus of material that is level-appropriate, you can work on increasing the depth of knowledge about new words using contexts with which learners will already be familiar. Tom Cobb at the Université du Québec à Montréal has created a free online corpus interface called *Compleat Lexical Tutor* (a simple Web search will find it). This allows you to load your own texts and offers a number of possible ways of using the data with your students. Online you can also access the Bank of English and do concordance and collocate searches. As with most concordance software, the facility allows you to blank out the search word. This could then be used as a guessing task.

Finally, we again stress the importance of encouraging your learners to keep vocabulary notebooks and the need to continually add new information about words as they encounter new meanings, new collocates and new colligational patterns.

Chapter review

1 What does colligation mean?

2 What does it mean to say that words have a paradigmatic relationship?

    a. They share a certain amount of meaning.

    b. They mean exactly the same thing.

    c. They are opposites.

    d. One word has taken its meaning from the other.

3 What does it mean to say that words have a syntagmatic relationship?

    a. They are always used together.

    b. They are connected through syntactic or grammatical patterns.

    c. They mean the same thing.

    d. One can be used instead of the other without changing the grammatical pattern.

4 Patterns differ across registers. Give an example of an order or command in the following registers:

    a. A parent to a child

    b. A boss to her secretary

    c. A public notice

    d. A colleague to another colleague

5 Here's an entry from a learner's vocabulary notebook for a new word. What colligational information could they add?

Mourn = feel or be very sad usually when someone close to you has died.

e.g. She mourned the death of her husband.

6 Which one of the following statements is true?

a. Learners need to learn all of the colligations of a word when they first encounter it.

b. Learners should learn colligational patterns before collocational patterns.

c. Learners will remember the word better if they know its colligations.

d. Learners shouldn't be expected to learn all the colligations of a word at once.

7 What is negative transfer?

8 What strategies can be used, even at Beginners' level, to promote colligational knowledge?

9 What kind of materials help learners find out about colligational patterns?

10 Why is important to have a level-appropriate corpus if you are working on colligational patterns using concordance lines?

5 | Multi-word items

As we have already seen in Chapters 1 and 2, when we start to describe words, we see that a 'word' can be represented in any number of ways:

- single items or basic roots: *table, door, lamp*
- compounds where two or more words are combined: *tabletop, door-handle, lampshade*
- lexical chunks with relatively fixed meanings: *at the end of the day, so on and so forth, to and fro*
- prepositional phrases: *at the moment, on the left, over and over*

It is clear, then, that we cannot always talk about words as single items. Instead, we must understand how combinations of words function to produce specific meanings. One such category of fixed forms is idioms which we will cover in Chapter 6.

Here, we will focus on compounds, prepositional phrases and lexical chunks. What characteristics do these vocabulary items have, what problems do they pose for learners and how might we go about teaching them?

Compounds

As you may remember from Chapter 1, a compound is simply a word that is made up of a root form and other 'add-ons', which may be other words or **affixes.** An affix simply refers to the additional 'bits' which we add at to the beginning or end of a word. For example, the word *unproblematic* is made up of the root *problem*, the prefix *un-*, and the suffix *-atic*. By combining these various elements, we can change both the form and meaning of a word; in this case, from the noun *problem* to the adjective *unproblematic*. Alternatively, we can combine a single root word with others to give different meanings: *word+list = wordlist, check+out = checkout,* and so on.

Affixation

English has a fairly limited number of affixes which can be used to make compounds and change a word's form or basic meaning. Some are relatively productive and allow many compounds to be generated.

Most native speakers are able to work out the meanings of words from their knowledge of affixes and it is clearly worth teaching learners how affixes function so they can work out the meanings of new words.

TASK 1

Complete the table below. Say what the function of each affix is and add one more example for each.

Affix and function	Examples
-ly (makes an adjective)	Quickly
non-	non-starter
in-	inconvenient
re-	recast
-ing	reading
de-	devalue
-s	boys

Compounding

In addition to using affixes to change the form or meaning of a word, we can also simply combine words:

noun + noun	handlebar, window-cleaner, keypad
adjective + noun	soft-spot, hardhat
verb + noun	grindstone, pushchair
verb + verb	make-do
verb + particle	get by, lean over
particle + noun	off-day, on-task, overdraw

Note that, from a learning and teaching point of view, most materials present compounds as single word items and do not 'break them down' into their constituent parts. There is strong evidence to suggest that we store and retrieve words as 'whole units' (See, for example, Lewis, 2002). The implication, then, is that this how they should be taught.

TASK 2

Give three examples of compounds for each combination below (15 words in total):

noun + noun
adjective + noun
verb + noun
verb + verb
verb + particle

TASK 3

To what extent do you feel a need to **deconstruct** words like the following in order to ascertain their meaning? What about learners? What strategies might be useful for teaching learners how to deal with such words?

Reproduce	*Irrefutable*
Unforgettable	*Photogenic*
Unimaginable	*Irresponsibility*

Prepositional phrases

There are many **prepositional phrases** in English which function as single word items. They usually comprise a preposition plus a noun phrase and often refer to place or time: *at the end of the day; from time to time; from here to eternity; for ever and ever.* Again, these are normally learnt as single items and are not usually broken down into their constituent parts. It is interesting to note that some of these phrases have both literal and idiomatic meanings, for example, *at the end of the day*, which can mean both 'as the day comes to an end' and 'in conclusion'.

Phrasal verbs

When we combine verbs with other grammatical words, such as adverbs, we create **phrasal verbs** such as *take off, put on, get out*, etc. Each phrasal verb consists of a verb (take), and a particle, normally a preposition or adverb (off). Phrasal verbs pose problems for learners for a number of reasons:

- there are so many of them and they have similar forms
- their meanings are often similar
- their meanings are often difficult to work out
- they occur in informal English, making them difficult to identify and understand.

A major difficulty is deciding which of the many phrasal verbs are the most useful to teach. Using corpora, we can find out which verbs occur most frequently. For example, the most frequent particles in phrasal verbs are *in, on, up, out, off, down, around, for, with*, and so on. These combine with the most frequent verbs such as *go, come, get, make, look, put*, etc. From this we can make a list of core, useful phrasal verbs for teaching which will include items such as *get on, get by, go on, look up, look around, make up, put in, put off*, and so forth (McCarthy et al., 2007).

Another difficulty is that meanings may be highly transparent or more context-specific. Consider *get on*, for example. Depending on the context, it can mean 'board' (*Mike got on the number 42 bus*), 'continue' (*get on with your work*), 'understand' (*you all need to get on together*), or 'leave' (*I'd better be getting on*). We can say, then, that some words are more opaque or transparent than others; their meanings are more obvious whether they appear in or out of context.

Some verbs can be separated from their particle, others cannot. Compare, for example:

---

work out: 'I worked out the answer myself' OR 'I worked the answer out myself'
get on: 'We're getting on fine now' BUT NOT 'We're getting fine on now'

TASK 4

Which of the following phrasal verbs are separable and which are not?

look around	get up to	put on	make do
look up	get on	put off	make off with
look at	get around to	put up to	make sure
look over	get off	put through	make over

Lexical chunks

In addition to compounds and prepositional phrases, there are many other multi-word units, or '**lexical chunks**' which are fixed or semi-fixed, and which we can treat as single words. There are different ways of classifying these, including:

- Discourse markers: *by the way, what's more, even so.*
- Social formulae (used to establish and maintain relations): *how's it going, see you soon, I was wondering if.*
- Sentence builders (used as 'a way into' a particular topic or subject): *the thing is, what I mean is, if you ask me.*

One advantage of lexical chunks for learners is that they can be learnt as single items, saving time and making recall faster. Some claim that learning and using chunks is an aid to fluency, allowing speakers and writers more time to clarify intended meaning or to seek clarification.

VOCABULARY FILE

Another advantage of lexical chunks is that they can be used to generate other phrases which have similar meanings: *see you later → see you soon → see you in a bit → see you next week,* and so on.

Some of the most frequently found chunks are used almost exclusively in spoken English, more specifically in conversations. Take *I think* and *you know*, for example.

When we look at spoken corpora, these chunks have a very high frequency because they perform specific functions. *I think* acts as a kind of hedge to soften what speakers are saying and to help them be less assertive, while *you know* creates 'shared space' between speakers, allowing greater informality and more equal roles.

Consider these examples:

(1)

[Discussing a successful football team]

A: *Is it the degree of talent that they have? Maybe the system that they've put in? Is it the coaching?*

B: *Well, I, **I think** it's a combination. There's no doubt that they have outstanding talent, **you know**.*

(2)

A: *So if you just go down to the fish market or the butcher or, **you know**, just your local supermarket and see what's on offer that day. And cook it – grill it up, and that's your dinner.*

In (1), Speaker B uses a combination of *I think* and *you know* to express an opinion, but also to soften that stance and present a more sympathetic point of view. Remove these chunks and the interaction immediately becomes less friendly, even hostile.

There are many other two-word chunks which are used in spoken language to help create successful interactions. These include *I mean, you see, I see,* and *I know* and are normally referred to as **discourse markers.** Clearly, learners must master these key chunks and understand how they function to help maintain the flow of a conversation.

Some of the more common words frequently occur in longer chunks. Take *know* for example. *Know* is used in four and five word chunks which have high frequencies and which are essential in spoken discourse. Consider the following examples taken from the COBUILD American spoken corpus:

- *Know what I mean?*
- *Do you know what I mean?*
- *Do you know what I'm saying?*
- *You know what I'm saying?*
- *I know what you mean.*

In each case, the function of the chunk is to maintain the flow of the interaction, keep the channels open and ensure that speaker and listener understand each other.

TASK 5

There are many examples of lexical chunks which are used to create and maintain relationships. These 'social formulae' can be quite confusing for learners and may even be misused. Which of the following would you teach to a group of adult, intermediate learners? Which would you omit and why?

How's tricks?	See you.
Have a good one.	Long time no see.
Nice to see you.	Better be going now.
What about you?	Catch you later.

Other high-frequency chunks include the following, again, all taken from the American spoken corpus:

WORD	FREQUENT CHUNKS
Time	for a time, at the time, a short time, a long time, most of the time
Way	the way things are going, the way home, change in the way, in the same way
End	at the end of, in the end, come to an end, by the end of, towards the end of
Thing	one thing that, this /that kind of thing, the same thing, the important thing is
Things	a lot of things, kinds of things, things like that, one of the things

Why chunks are important

Including common chunks in the notion of 'vocabulary' has some important consequences for learning English:

- We begin to look at vocabulary as consisting of more than just single words and collocating pairs of words.
- In spoken language especially, some of the most common chunks have important interactive functions (hedging or calling on shared knowledge, for example).
- The most common chunks help to create successful communication.
- Ready-made chunks enable us to be fluent. We do not have to create them anew every time we need them (see Wray, 2000, 2002).
- If learners can learn and retrieve the most useful chunks, they will sound more fluent.

(McCarthy et al., 2007)

Binomials and trinomials

English also has a number of pairs (**binomials**) and trios (**trinomials**) of words which are fixed both syntactically and semantically; that is, both the word order and meaning are invariable. Examples include:

Binomials
to and fro
black and white
salt and pepper
fish and chips
sick and tired

Trinomials
cool, calm and collected
hook, line and sinker
left, right and centre
ready, willing and able
(McCarthy, 1990)

Clearly, the implication for learners is that these have to be learnt and used as single items. Breaking such fixed phrases down into their constituent parts is only going to cause confusion and slow down the learning process. As Palmer said many years ago (1925) when giving advice about oral fluency, 'memorise perfectly the largest number of common and useful word groups'. (See also Chapter 1).

PART B What are the problems for learners?

There are several difficulties for learners associated with multi-word items:

1 Transparency of meaning. We've already seen that the meanings of some multi-word items are straightforward and literal, while others are more difficult to predict, even from context. For example, many phrasal and prepositional verbs have to be learnt as their meaning cannot be worked out, even from context. Examples include *to be out on a limb, to be on the ball.*

2 Fixedness. Some items are totally fixed and cannot be changed at all, while others can generate similar expressions (as in greetings, for example, *see you, see you later, see you next week* and so on). For learners, it is difficult to learn the extent to which an item is fixed or variable.

3 Frequency and usefulness. Depending on the context where learning is taking place, some items will have more relevance than others. For example, the greeting *What about you?* is very common in Northern Ireland and learners there would find it useful. However, it is not widely used in other contexts and could therefore be ignored.

4 Pronunciation. Sentence stress and rhythm are key to correct pronunciation of multi-word units. For example, the binomial *black and white* has to stress 'black' and 'white', while 'and' is practically 'thrown away'. Learners need to understand this principle at an early stage if they are to master correct pronunciation. Similarly, the word stress in compounds may cause some difficulty for learners when they encounter a word for the first time. How can learners know where to place the stress on a word they come across for the first time?

5 Syntax. The word order of multi-word units is normally fixed and cannot be varied. We normally say *boys and girls,* not *girls and boys,* or *fish and chips,* not *chips and fish,* and so on. A learner's ability to master the exact word order is key to their ability to sound more like a native speaker.

6 Guessing meaning from context. As we've seen in the earlier part of this chapter, some fixed expressions are difficult to predict even when they are used in context. For example, what clues can learners use to guess the meanings of the following phrases?

Long time no see

*She always has to **make a scene***

*I just don't know **which way to turn***

Why might the following items present difficulties for learners? Translate them into another language that you are familiar with. What differences do you see between the two languages in terms of words used, word order and literal meanings?

Forever and a day
Get on with
Make it up
Kinds of things
By the end of
At the time

PART C How do we teach it?

Context and level

Teaching multi-word items will obviously depend on both context and level. With advanced learners, a more inductive approach can be adopted, whereby learners are left to work things out on their own. With lower levels, teachers will need to offer more support and guidance and check form, function and pronunciation.

Form	What grammatical features need to be observed (for example, the use of prepositions, verb form, and so on)?
Function	What does the item mean and how can meaning be checked?
Pronunciation	What is the most natural pronunciation, which key words need to be stressed, which can be 'thrown away', unstressed?

Take the very common phrase *at the end of the day*, for example. Learners will have encountered all of these words individually before, but what special features do they need to notice in this phrase? First of all, the use of prepositions *at* and *of* (we don't say *in* the end of the day, for example) and the definite article *the*. Secondly, they should notice the specific meaning, 'in conclusion' or 'when all's said and done'. Finally, the pronunciation: put stress on *end* and *day*; 'throw away' *at* and *the;* and note the linking between *end* and *of*.

Look at the extract below from a pre-intermediate, adult ESL class. How well does this teacher teach *in a penalty shoot-out*? Consider the points made above and suggest ways in which this might have been done better.

81	T	now … see if you can find the words that are suitable in these phrases (reading) in the world cup final of 1994 Brazil Italy 2 3 2 and in a shoot-out … what words would you put in there? ((1))
82	L7	[beat]
83	T	[what] beat Italy 3 2 yeah in?
84	L7:	in a penalty shoot-out
85	T	a what?
86	L7:	in a penalty shoot-out
87	T	in a penalty shoot-out very good in a penalty shoot-out

(Walsh, 2001)

In the extract below, the teacher is working with a group of upper-intermediate, adult, ESL learners. Notice how she guides them to the meaning and use of *roller skating*.

(a) How does she 'scaffold' (feed in linguistic support) the word that L5 is looking for?

(b) How does she model the correct use of the word?

(c) How does she repair learners' contributions (correct errors)?

218	L5:	the good news is he went to the went to
219	T:	he went to what do we call these things the shoes with wheels
220	L2:	ah skates
221	L6:	roller skates
222	T:	ROLler skates roller skates so [he went]
223	L5:	[he went] to
224	L:	roller SKATing
225	T:	SKATing
226	L5:	he went to
227	T:	not to just he went [roller skating he went roller skating]
228	L5:	[roller skating he went roller skating]

Vocabulary selection

As well as thinking about context and level, and in relation to both, teachers need to pay attention to vocabulary selection, focusing on high frequency words and giving learners strategies to deal with low frequency words. This is where a corpus can be extremely useful in deciding on which words to teach and to which level.

TASK 9

Look again at the frequency lists for some of the most frequently occurring chunks, taken from the American spoken corpus in COBUILD. Which chunks would you select for a low-intermediate group, which for an advanced group? How did you decide?

WORD	FREQUENT CHUNKS
Time	for a time, at the time, a short time, a long time, most of the time
Way	the way things are going, the way home, change in the way, in the same way
End	at the end of, in the end, come to an end, by the end of, towards the end of
Thing	one thing that, this/that kind of thing, the same thing, the important thing is
Things	a lot of things, kinds of things, things like that, one of the things

---

In this chapter, we have seen that a 'word' can be represented in any number of ways. It can be a single item (pen), a compound (light-switch), a lexical chunk (fish and chips), or a prepositional phrase (in a few minutes). Combinations of words may be more or less fixed, transparent or context dependent. We need to look beyond individual words and see how words combine when analysing language for teaching.

Chapter review

1   In the following compounds, identify the root word and each affix. Complete the table as fully as possible.

Word	Root	Affix(es)
Photographic		
Countries		
Disappointment		
Redundancy		
Irrelevance		

2 To what extent do you think that we should break more complex words into their constituent parts for teaching purposes?

3 Why do phrasal verbs create problems for learners?

4 For each of the following verbs, how many different meanings can you identify? What are the implications for teaching?

To go off

To get by

To make do

To put up

To get through

5 Why should we teach lexical chunks? More than one answer is correct.

a. We find repeated patterns that contribute to fluency.

b. Chunks help to increase formality between speaker and listener.

c. Chunks contain mainly content words.

d. Chunks may be easier to remember and retrieve than single words.

6 In teaching, what are the three most important things to think about when dealing with chunks?

7 What are the underlined parts of these words called and why are they important:

<u>un</u>important   laugh<u>able</u>   manage<u>ment</u>

8 How many 'words' (compounds, lexical chunks, prepositional phrases) can you make from the following words?

Desk

Shoe

Cup

Tip

9 How many other chunks can you find like the ones below?

Time	for a time, at the time,
Way	change in the way, in the same way
End	at the end of, in the end,

10 Look at the chunks in Question 9. Which ones would you select to teach at a low-intermediate level?

6 | Idioms

What is an idiom?

TASK 1

What is the difference in meaning between sentence A and B in each pair?

(1)	A	He hit the sack with a stick but it seemed to be empty.
	B	He hit the sack at 10 o'clock and was asleep by 10.15.
(2)	A	She wore a red glove on her left hand, and on the other hand she wore a blue glove.
	B	She's very famous, but on the other hand, she's very natural, normal and friendly.
(3)	A	He went to the wall and climbed over it into the garden.
	B	A lot of small businesses have gone to the wall because of the economic crisis.

Sometimes, we can understand expressions simply by looking at the meaning of each individual word in them. So, as long as I know the words *ship, sink deep* and *water*, I can understand the sentence, *The ship sank in deep water*. But what about these sentences:

My heart sank when I heard the news.
We're going to be in deep water if the company doesn't make a profit this year.

Even if we know the words in the sentences, we need to know more. We need to know that if your heart sinks, you do not feel tired, you do not die of a heart attack, but you do feel sad or worried (like, for example, when you hear bad news). And in the second sentence, you need to know that deep water has nothing to do with getting wet or standing in a pool, but means being in a difficult situation. It may help us to understand the non-literal meaning of the sentence if we understand the individual words, but not always. In these sentences, the words give us no clue as to what the expressions in bold-type mean:

You'll just have to **keep your nose to the grindstone**.
His old uncle **kicked the bucket** *a couple of months ago.*

We either know what the expressions in bold mean or we have to work very hard indeed to interpret what they mean in the context. *Keep your nose to the grindstone* (meaning to continue to work hard without stopping) and *kick the bucket* (meaning to die) are **idioms.**

Some idioms are easier to understand than others; they are more or less transparent. The expression, *That's news to me!,* is not too difficult to understand: it means 'that is information that surprises me!'; it is relatively transparent. The expression *to have (several) irons in the fire* is much more difficult to understand. Does it mean to have problems, to have dreams or ambitions, to have powers or abilities? In fact it means to have several jobs at the same time, or job possibilities. *To have irons in the fire* is opaque (the opposite of transparent). Idioms can be placed on a scale, from more transparent to more opaque. Here are some examples of idiomatic expressions with the word *hand*:

give someone a hand	(help them)
force someone's hand	(make them do something)
get out of hand	(get out of control)
be a dab hand	(be very skilled at something)

The other important characteristic is that idioms are usually very fixed in their form. The expression *to keep one's nose to the grindstone* (see above) always has that form: we cannot say hold *your nose …* or *stick your nose …,* we cannot say keep your nose *on* or *at* the grindstone, we cannot say *millstone* or *tombstone* instead of *grindstone*. We normally never use the expression in the plural or in the passive (for example, we don't normally say *Noses were kept to the grindstone all day*). Similarly, we don't say *The bucket was kicked by his old uncle and he inherited a fortune.* The idiom *to be barking up the wrong tree* (meaning to be wrong in the way you do something or think about something) is always used in the continuous form – we never say *She barked up the wrong tree*. However, some idioms are more flexible than others. As well as saying *give someone a hand*, we can say *lend someone a hand*. We can say *hit the nail on the head* (meaning to state exactly the reason for a problem) and we can strengthen it by saying *hit the nail <u>right</u> on the head*. As well as saying *get the sack* (be dismissed from your job), we can say *give someone the sack* (dismiss them). The expression *to pass the buck* (meaning to pass the responsibility you have for something to another person to avoid tackling the problem) can be used in the active or passive:

*Politicians are always **passing the buck** and not taking responsibility for their actions.*
***The buck was passed** from one ministry to another – no-one wanted to accept responsibility.*

Native speakers and expert users of English know thousands of idiomatic expressions; they know what they mean, they know what restrictions there are on the forms they can be used in and how flexible they are.

What different types of idioms are there?

TASK 2

Many of the idioms we have looked at so far consist of a verb and an object (for example, *kick the bucket, pass the buck, hit the sack, force someone's hand*). What do the pairs of idioms in bold have in common?

*I ran **to and fro** all morning.*	*You have to accept **the ups and downs** of life.*
*I will be **on hand** if you need me.*	*I'm **out of touch** with the latest pop music.*
*I'm **ready, willing and able** to do anything to help.*	*They sold the company **lock, stock and barrel**.*
*He's **as thin as a rake**.*	*She was **as keen as mustard**.*

One way of classifying idioms is to look at their grammar. There are a number of different types of idiom in terms of grammatical form. Here are some of the most common types:

Type	Example
verb + object	kick the bucket, pass the buck
prepositional phrase	on the go, off the wall
binomial	give and take, off and on, sink or swim
trinomial	lock, stock and barrel, cool, calm and collected
frozen similes	as quiet as a mouse, as strong as an ox
possessive expressions	the bee's knees, the lion's share, a king's ransom
idiomatic compounds	the happy hour, a mish-mash, to make do

As we can see, idioms come in many forms, and although some are relatively infrequent and few in number (for example the trinomials and the possessive expressions), some are frequent and great in number (such as prepositional phrase idioms).

How frequent are idioms in everyday language?

Compared with common single words and compared with the most frequent chunks (see Chapter 8), the idioms we have looked at so far are relatively infrequent, though some are much more frequent than others. In a sample of almost 55 million words of texts from British books in the Bank of English corpus, the idioms with *hand* which we saw above are distributed as follows:

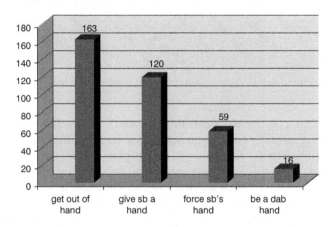

The most frequent among our selection of 'hand' idioms, *get out of hand*, is ten times more common than the least frequent, *be a dab hand*. But the expression *on the other hand* actually occurs 2719 times in the same corpus, which is 170 times more frequent than *be a dab hand*! Some of the other idioms we have mentioned in this chapter are relatively infrequent in the same 50-million word corpus, occurring only 20 times or less:

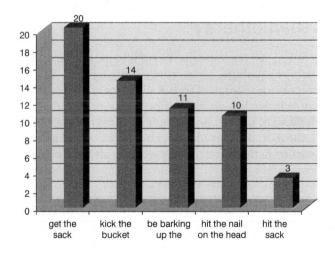

To get some idea of how infrequent these idioms are, we can intersperse them with words of similar frequencies from our British books sample from the Bank of English:

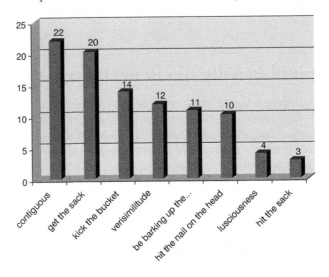

Words such as *contiguous, verisimilitude* and *lusciousness* would all be considered very rare words and very advanced for learners of English, and yet their frequency is similar to the idioms we saw in Figure 6.3. So we can see, by looking at a corpus, that many idiomatic expressions are very infrequent indeed, compared with the everyday words we need to teach our language learners. However, O'Keeffe et al. (2006: 85) give lists of idioms which are relatively frequent from a selection of 200 idioms extracted manually from British and North American spoken corpora (100 idioms from each variety), and claim that the frequency of their selected items is similar to that of words at the 5000–7000 word level which an upper intermediate or advanced level learner might be expected to understand.

Are some words more likely to occur in idioms than others?

So far, we have looked at a random selection of idioms. But can we organise idioms in any way? Are there any patterns, apart from classifying them into grammatical types (for example, prepositional phrases, verb + object expressions and so on), as we did above? Some words in English do seem to be 'idiom-prone', that is to say they form the basis of a whole set of idioms. An example is words to do with parts of the human body. The hand, the foot, the eyes and other body parts all act as key words in idioms. For example, apart from the 'hand' idioms we have already looked at, we also have:

put one's foot in it	catch someone's eye	keep an eye on
get off on the wrong foot	cast an eye over	in one's mind's eye
put one's foot down	have an eye for something	look someone in the eye
shoot oneself in the foot	see eye to eye	an eye-opener

So, one way we can group idioms is by the key words they are based on. This could be, as we have seen, parts of the body, or particular animals (*let the cat out of the bag, play cat and mouse, fight like cat and dog*), or common adjectives such as *hot* (*hot off the press, all hot and bothered, be in hot water*), and so on. McCarthy and O'Dell (2002) group idioms according to key words, with many centring around body parts, common nouns such as *line, act, action* and *activity*, and adjectives such as *good* and *bad*.

Another way of grouping idioms is according to themes or topic areas. The *Cambridge International Dictionary of Idioms* (1998) has a special section of idioms classified according to themes such as 'anger', 'intelligence and stupidity', 'success and failure', and so on. This underlines the particular usefulness of special idioms dictionaries for learners, where the lexicographers have given a great deal of attention to how best to organise the thousands of idioms they present for learners. The *Longman Idioms Dictionary* (1998) contains more than 6000 idioms, while the *Oxford Idioms Dictionary for Learners of English* (2006) has some 10 000 idioms in current use in English – a formidable learning task and one where any help given in organising this mass of information is invaluable. The Oxford dictionary, for example, includes study pages exploring common themes (such as idioms that describe types of people, or the way people look). All the idioms dictionaries mentioned here are based on corpora, so that learners can be confident that the idioms in the dictionaries are in current usage, and the dictionaries often indicate which idioms are the most common.

What do idioms mean and how do people use them?

TASK 3

Why do you think speaker B uses the idiom in bold-type in this conversation?

A:	This economic crisis is terrible, everyone's losing money and people are losing their jobs.
B:	Yes, and whose fault is it?
A:	Well, it's the bankers and the politicians, but they never seem to take responsibility for it all.
B:	Yes, that's right. They're always **passing the buck!**

Idioms have figurative (non-literal) meanings. These meanings have developed and become 'fossilised' over long periods of time. There may have been a time when some of the more opaque idioms had transparent, literal meanings. The idiom *to kick over the traces*, for example, which means in modern English to act in a way that shows no respect for authority, came originally from the time when vehicles and farm equipment were pulled by horses. The traces were leather straps used to tie a horse to a plough or a cart or other vehicle. If the horse kicked and got its feet tangled over the straps, it was out of control. Very few people now know the literal, transparent meaning; for most people, the idiom is just an opaque expression whose meaning they know as one whole unit. However, the colourful imagery of the original meanings of many idioms still remains, and there is evidence to suggest that we process them at least in part – and in the first few moments that we hear or read them – by thinking of the literal meaning, or else that we process literal and non-literal meanings in parallel with one another. Everything seems to depend on which meanings of the words are most **salient** or prominent. The literal meaning may be salient (that is, more accessible to us because of frequency and familiarity), or, equally, the non-literal meaning may be salient and familiar to us, enabling us to jump straight to a figurative interpretation (Giora, 2003). In the debate on the power of salient meanings, it is not always clear how influential the context is in forcing our interpretations, but context undoubtedly plays an important role. For language learners, as we shall see below, the processing challenges may be different. However, some linguists think that universal metaphors often underlie idioms and that such metaphors are the key to understanding idiomatic expressions, especially where they are shared across languages (Charteris-Black, 2002).

But what are idioms for? Why do we seem to have two ways of saying many things? Why do we have *die* and *kick the bucket*, *go to bed* and *hit the sack*, and so on? Clearly, the figurative meanings say more than just what happens, or how something is, in an objective way. They are subjective and evaluative; they are often colourful and humorous, and, in the case of **frozen similes**, binomials and trinomials (see Chapter 5), they seem to have a rhythm and musicality which sets them apart from their literal equivalents.

Compare:

He's a complete charlatan! He's an out and out charlatan! (repetition of *out*)
She has poor eyesight. She's as blind as a bat. (repetition of /b/ sound)

When we look at how idioms are actually used in a corpus, we see the evaluative function coming out strongly. For example, we often find them at the end of a segment of text, when the speaker or writer is summing up or evaluating a series of events or an argument. In this extract from a conversation, note how speaker B uses the idiomatic compound *a small world* to sum up the coincidence that has just come to light:

A: *No I'm not from Manchester. I'm from Leeds.*
B: *Yeah me too.*
A: *What a coincidence! Are you from Leeds too?*
B: *Yeah.*
A: *Oh my gosh!*
B: *Isn't it **a small world!***
A: *Yeah, it is.*

In the next extract from a conversation about having to pay an excessive sum of money for a garden designer's services, speaker A uses two idioms. He first criticises the poor value for money by suggesting that the designer did his work in a very careless way (using the idiom *on the back of an envelope*, meaning to design or plan something in a very informal and hasty way), then sums up the experience using the idiom to *learn one's lesson the hard way* (meaning to learn something about life through a bad experience):

A: *This garden designer charged me a fee of £2000 for what he'd done, and it was all **on the back of an envelope**.*
B: *Wow!*
A: *I **learnt my lesson the hard way**.*
B: *Mm. You sure did!*

Evaluating an event or situation in this way is a very common function of idioms (McCarthy, 1998). What we often find, as in the two examples above, is that the speaker(s) or writer recounts or describes something using literal language, then sums it up or repeats it in part using an idiom. In this way, idioms are often surrounded by strong clues to their meaning in the immediate context. Idioms, therefore, are not neutral; they are not simply duplicates of their literal equivalents, but perform important evaluative functions in the language. O'Keeffe et al. (2006: Chapter 4) give many more examples of idioms in evaluative contexts.

Finally we should note that idioms occur not just in everyday, informal contexts, but also in specialist registers such as business English and academic English. O'Keeffe et al. (2006) give examples from a spoken business English corpus, and Simpson and Mendis (2003) show how idioms are used widely in a spoken academic corpus (the MICASE corpus).

PART B What are the problems for learners?

TASK 4

What problems do you think learners might have in using these English idioms?

A shot in the dark
To put your foot in it

Idioms seem to present learners with an impossible mountain to climb. Advanced, expert non-native users of English still have problems with idioms, even when they have achieved large vocabularies and an impressive, accurate command of grammar. Many studies have shown errors in the use of idioms by learners in terms of both form and function, as well as under-use of idioms in comparison with native-speaker use, or avoidance of idioms in favour of more literal alternatives (Kellerman, 1986; Yorio, 1989; Arnaud and Savignon, 1997). Because of their different degrees of flexibility, and because of their often specialised meanings and functions, idioms are very difficult to understand and particularly difficult to use correctly. What is more, as Irujo (1986) suggests, idioms can seem strange when learners and other non-native users write or speak them – it is as if idioms belong to the native speakers of the language as a 'badge of membership'.

One immediate and most obvious problem for learners is the sheer number of opaque idioms in the language, running into many hundreds. How does a learner know when an expression is an idiom, and how do they know what the idiom means? One possibility is that an identical or similar idiom exists in the learner's first language (L1). Irujo (1986) suggested that identical idioms as between L1 and L2 (the target language) were the easiest for learners to comprehend and produce. Idioms which were similar but not identical were more problematic – they were easy to understand, but more difficult to produce accurately in L2. Idioms which were opaque, that is, where there was the biggest difference between the literal meaning and the figurative meaning, were even more difficult for learners to comprehend

(Cooper, 1999). Saliency (in terms of familiarity with the idioms, for example, that learners had already heard them or come across them) seems to help. Also, the lack of flexibility of idioms may actually be to learners' advantage.

Learners do seem to use the context, where it is available to them, to interpret expressions that seem to make no sense in their L1. However, sometimes they try to translate idioms into their L1 and this can cause problems of **negative transfer.**

In Chapter 3, we mentioned that learners often process language 'bottom-up', that is to say they process it word by word, and struggle to make sense of stretches of language where individual words seem to make no sense in the overall discourse. This is likely to be a particular problem for the processing of idioms, especially for beginning learners. And even for the more advanced learner who develops skills of processing language 'top-down', that is to say, looking at longer stretches of language and getting meaning from whole phrases, collocations, chunks or idioms or even whole sentences in one go, there are still big problems. How common or rare is the idiom in question? Is it informal and colloquial, or can it be used in most situations? Is it associated with a special register, such as journalism or advertising? These are all questions which we need to tackle when we are considering how and what to teach about idioms.

PART C How do we teach it?

The first concern as regards teaching idioms must be at what level do we start to introduce them? Given that so many idioms are relatively rare, and that so many are relatively opaque in their meaning, can we do anything for learners at lower levels, or do we simply wait until the advanced level? In Chapter 1, we suggested that the top priority in vocabulary learning at the elementary level must be mastering the first 2000 words, since they work harder than all the other words in the language. In Chapter 7, we shall suggest that certain everyday common chunks should be given priority at an early stage, so there seems to be a strong case for leaving idioms until the intermediate level. One possibility is to gradually take learners from the single-word stage to an understanding of longer stretches of language. This can be done by starting with some of the words which we mentioned as being 'idiom-prone'. For example, most learners learn the names of the parts of the human body quite early on in their studies. Based on a word such as *hand*, we can take learners first to common collocations and chunks such as *(on the) left/right hand (side)*, *hand someone a book/pen/piece of paper*, to common idioms such as *on the other hand* and *give someone a hand*. This process of taking learners 'from word to idiom' helps to develop their language awareness as well as increasing their multi-word vocabulary.

Most important of all is not to teach obscure idioms which are very rare, because not only will learners probably never see them again, if they use them, they may sound very strange or even ridiculous. This means that dictionaries and teaching materials should be evaluated by the extent to which the information in them is up to date and reliable, and what this means in practice is whether a corpus has been used or not, or at least whether the idioms chosen are based on proper observation of what people use, when and how. The *Cambridge International Dictionary of Idioms* (1998) very visibly highlights the most common idioms, based on a large corpus, so teachers and learners know that those particular idioms are frequent and useful. There are also corpus-based self-study materials. McCarthy and O'Dell (2002) base their selection of idioms on a large corpus and group the idioms in various ways that attempt to organise them for learners (based on familiar key words; everyday concepts such as time, animals, war; and idioms for talking about common topics such as health, danger, happiness and sadness, and so on).

VOCABULARY FILE

For more advanced level learners, data-driven learning (where learners are directly exposed to corpus data, usually in the form of concordances) may be a good way of looking at idioms in context.

And for learners in specialised areas, concordances and lists of idioms used in those special areas, based on corpus data, may be a very fast and efficient way of training learners into the discourse of their chosen professional area (Simpson and Mendis, 2003).

As we saw with collocation in Chapter 3, developing language awareness may be the best course of action for understanding what idioms are, how people use them, discussing – perhaps through one's own language and looking at data – why idioms are being used and what the problems are in understanding and using them for learners. Teachers should not hesitate to use learners' knowledge of their L1 to develop language awareness. Spöttl and McCarthy (2004) present evidence that the L1 does play a role in the processing of collocations, chunks and idioms; teachers can discuss the problems of transfer between languages with more advanced learners. The idioms practice material in McLay (1987), for example, gives L1 cues to speakers of some European languages to assist them in selecting the right English idiom. The discussion with learners should also include considerations about whether idioms are best learnt just for understanding (**receptive use**) or actively (**productive use**).

We have looked at both form and meaning in this chapter, and teaching should ideally focus on both. Because it is likely that learners may, at least initially, pick up literal meanings from idiomatic expressions, there may be good reasons to exploit those literal meanings in class. Boers (2007), for example, argues that the meaning of many idioms is connected with their original, literal usage, and that associating an idiom with its original, literal meaning can promote good learning and retention of the idiom. The original, literal association can create a clear mental image of a scene in the learner's mind, which the learner can store in memory alongside the form of the idiom.

Other applied linguists and materials writers have tried to organise idioms for learners in terms of form and function and meaning. Lattey (1986) suggests that idioms can be organised on the basis of the contexts in which they are used, for example, interaction of the speaker and listener, the speaker and the outside world, evaluations of people and things, and so on. Wright (1999) organises some of his material for teaching idioms around metaphors based on parts of the body and other universal metaphors such as 'Life is a journey' and 'Business is war'. As we mentioned in Part B, universal metaphors may be a powerful organising feature for idioms.

Idioms often occur at the end of stories (McCarthy, 1998), and encouraging learners to associate idioms with their own experiences through story-telling or other personalisation activities may help them to learn them more efficiently (Bergstrom 1979). McCarthy et al. (2006: 100) present idioms in a story-telling context and grouping idioms according to the different stages of a story.

Finally, we should not underestimate the power of idioms simply to bring a little bit of fun into the classroom. Good learners are naturally curious, and we should not stifle or discourage that curiosity about any aspect of language. Teachers can encourage students to be creative with idioms in class, to have fun with them. And as long as there is the parallel awareness that one should be careful with their use out of class or in test situations, then idioms can form a natural part of vocabulary teaching and learning from the intermediate level onwards.

Chapter review

1   Which definition of an idiom is correct? Circle your answer.

    a. An idiom is a word that has a non-literal meaning which is only clear in context.

    b. An idiom is an expression whose meaning is more than the sum of the individual words.

    c. An idiom is an expression consisting of more than one word whose meaning is literal.

    d. An idiom is another term for a collocation, but it contains more than two words.

2   Which of these sentences contain idioms? Circle your answers.

    a. My sister works for a computer company.

    b. Our plan worked like clockwork.

    c. Give me a hand with this box, please.

    d. (to a child) Give me your hand so we can cross the road safely.

    e. No-one else had any money, so I had to foot the bill.

3   Put each idiom into the correct box.

out of touch
down and out
cool, calm and collected
a vicious circle
the cat's whiskers
burn your bridges
as dead as a doornail

possessive	binomial	verb+object	prepositional	trinomial	compound	simile

4 Only one of these statements is true. Which one?

   a. Most idioms are very frequent.

   b. Binomials are more frequent than trinomials.

   c. All idioms are completely fixed in their form.

   d. All idioms are flexible in their form.

5 Which of these words are idiom-prone? Put a tick (✔) for yes, a cross (✘) for no.

Eye _____

Rucksack _____

Printer _____

Hand _____

Cat _____

6 Which statements are true? Write **T** (true) or **F** (false).

   a. Idioms don't fall into groups. They are all very different. _____

   b. We can group idioms by their form, but not by topics. _____

   c. We can group idioms by topics (e.g. anger, happiness). _____

   d. Some animal names (e.g. dog, lion, horse) are the basis of idioms. _____

7 Why is salient meaning important in the way we process idioms? Circle the best answer.

   a. If the salient meaning is literal, some of the literal meaning comes to our mind before the idiomatic meaning.

   b. If the salient meaning is non-literal, we will immediately start thinking of the literal meaning.

   c. Because we need to have both the literal and non-literal meaning in our mind to understand an idiom.

8 True (**T**) or False (**F**)?

   a. Most linguists think that universal metaphors do not exist. _____

   b. All linguists believe that all idioms are always based on universal metaphors. _____

   c. Some linguists believe that there are often universal metaphors which can explain idioms. _____

9 Tick (✔) which of these statements are true of idioms in general.

   a. They are often colourful.

   b. They are often humorous.

   c. They are always formal.

   d. They are always completely opaque.

   e. They are often used to evaluate events.

   f. They mostly as frequent as everyday core words.

10 Put each idiom into the correct box for the special type of English it is associated with.

drive a hard bargain

top the charts

a last-ditch attempt

one-click purchasing

journalism	business	computers	music

7 | Word relations

What are word relationships?

TASK 1

Sort the following words into pairs or groups. Think about how you made your decisions.

cold   hot

great   apples

wonderful   pears

bank (of a river)   bananas

bank (where you put your money)

As we discussed in Chapter 2, words are signifiers of meaning. The relationship between a word and its meaning is an arbitrary one. Meanings evolve and change over time within groups of users. In Chapter 2, we touched on the 'sense relations' which some words have with others. This is a relationship of meaning rather than of grammar. For example, from Task 1, you will have grouped *great* and *wonderful* because they both express similar positive attributes. You will have paired off *hot* and *cold* because of their oppositeness of meaning. *Apples, pears, bananas,* you will have grouped together because they belong to the same category of *fruit*. And the *bank* of a river and the *bank* where you put your money are related because the words look and sound the same. All of these types of relationships will be explored in greater detail in this chapter.

Sense relations are both an aid to teaching vocabulary and an aid to memorising new words.

Teachers can draw on sense relationships when teaching new meanings. For example, when you are teaching *hawk* you are likely to draw on its category of bird, and when you teach *high*, it is helpful explain it with reference to its opposite *low*. If you are trying to explain the word *devastated*, you are likely to use a synonym such as *sad* in your explanation (we'll discuss synonyms in the next section). All of these strategies help your learners make semantic connections and these connections ultimately aid memory.

Another type of relationship which we will explore in this chapter is a type of extended meaning. This is when words are not used in their literal meaning, but they are used in an extended non-literal way to explain something in a comparative relationship. This is called **metaphoric** meaning. In this example, the underlined words or phrases are not used in their literal meaning:

> Rachel's rejection felt like <u>a knife in the heart</u> for him. Her <u>icy</u> words would stay with him for many years. She had <u>hurt</u> him very badly and there and then he felt that the <u>wounds</u> would never <u>heal</u>.

As you read this, you did not think that Rachel really put a knife in her lover's heart or that her words were made of ice. You did not think that she actually caused physical hurt to him or that there were actual wounds as a result. We understand the use of these words in this context as being non-literal or metaphoric. They express the shock and pain of an event very powerfully and very vividly. For learners of a language, metaphor can pose quite a challenge. In some instances, learners may not immediately recognise certain words or phrases as being non-literal in meaning. Metaphor is often associated with literary styles but we also use metaphor in every day language and it is something that we need to make our learners aware of.

What types of word relationships are there?

Synonymy

Where two or more words have the same meaning, that is, where one can substitute for the other without altering the meaning, we say that they are **synonyms** or that one is synonymous with the other. For example, *start* and *begin*, *worried* and *concerned*, *complete*, *end* and *finish*, and so on. Synonyms can be very useful in the teaching of meaning because we can draw on words of equivalent meaning which our students already know.

As you will have seen, the definition of *concur* draws on the more commonly used synonym *agree*, and *confab* makes use of the synonym *conversation* in its definition. *Contradictory* draws on the word *opposite* and the explanation of *contrite* uses the synonym *sorry*. In all of these cases, lesser known words have been explained by using more commonly known synonyms.

However, we need to be aware of the pitfalls of synonymy. There is rarely a one-to-one relationship between words. We usually only have 100 per cent synonymy with words which are used in different varieties of a language. Some examples of these are:

British English	American English
boot (of a car)	*trunk*
kerb	*sidewalk*
trailer	*caravan*
mobile phone	*cell phone*
biscuit	*cookie*

Going back to the synonyms from the definitions in Task 2, we can see that they are not 100 per cent synonyms:

Concur and *agree* lack 100 per cent synonymy because of register. *Concur* is more formal than *agree*. Regarding *confab* and *conversation*, *confab* is a very informal private talk between two people, whereas *conversation* is a neutral word. Equally, in the case of *contrite* and *sorry,* the latter is used in more formal registers whereas *sorry* is less formal and has a wider range of uses. Looking at *contradictory* and *opposite* in a little more detail, they do not have a 100 per cent relationship of synonym either, because they do not collocate with the same words. We cannot say:

He wanted to meet members of the contradictory sex.
They stood at contradictory sides of the room.
I walked in the contradictory direction.

Another type of relationship of equivalence or synonym is that of **cognates.** That is, where one word means the same in another language. In English, many words have been borrowed from other languages (see Chapter 1) and many of these mean exactly the same in English as they do in the language from which they originated. Many words in English have come from Latin and French and these are often written and pronounced similarly in other European languages:

English	French	Spanish	Italian	Portuguese
important	*important(e)*	*importante*	*importante*	*importante*
apartment	*appartement*	*apartamento*	*appartamento*	*apartamento*
intelligent	*intelligent(e)*	*inteligente*	*intelligente*	*inteligente*

There are many more cognates between English and these languages, as well as other languages which are related to English such as German, Dutch, Swedish and Norwegian. These cognates obviously give learners an advantage but there is a downside. Not all words that look or sound alike have the same meanings across languages. Therefore cognates can be tricky for learners. We will return to this in Part B.

Antonymy

An antonym is a word opposite in meaning.

TASK 3

What are the antonyms of the following words?

wet _____   thoughtful _____

light _____   kind _____

bright _____   give _____

happy _____   blow _____

rich _____   push _____

As with synonymy, this sense relationship of oppositeness can be very useful in the teaching of meaning. For example, if we are explaining the meaning of *ill*, it is helpful to explain that it means the opposite of *well* or *healthy*. When we teach *far*, it helps to explain it relative to its antonym *near*, and so on.

TASK 4

Provide more than one antonym for each of the following words.

light _____   rough _____

As you can see from Task 4, words can have more than one antonym and very often they differ in meaning because they are used in different contexts (or they are polysemic, see below and Chapter 4). In Task 4, you will have come up with more than one antonym for *light* and *rough*. Some possible answers:

*The suitcase was very light/**heavy**.*
*Her hair was a light/**dark** brown.*
*This bread is light/**fattening**.*

In the case of *rough*, you may have come up with some of the following antonyms:

*His hands were very rough/**smooth**.*
*The sea was rough/**calm**.*
*Jamie is such a rough/**gentle** boy.*

This poses a challenge when teaching meaning. If we teach students that the opposite of *rough* is *smooth*, then it could generate an error by over-generalisation, for example *The sea was smooth* or *Jamie is such a smooth boy*. Teaching antonyms in context and focusing on their collocations is important in overcoming this obstacle. We will also return to this in Part B.

Hyponyms

Hyponymy is a relationship of inclusion. It helps us to organise words into inclusive hierarchical relationships.

TASK 5

Fill in the blanks.

a. _____ is a type of animal.

b. _____ is a type of house.

c. _____ is a type of hat.

d. _____ is a type of shoe.

There are many possible answers to Task 5. Cat, dog, mouse, horse, pig, lion, cheetah, and so on are types of animal. Mansion, chalet, cabin, bungalow, semi-detached, detached, and so on are all types of houses. Stetson, trilby, pillbox, beret, bowler are all types of hats. Stiletto, platform, sandal, pump, mule are types of shoes.

In each case, what you have suggested to fill the blanks in Task 5 can be called a *hyponym*. Therefore, we can say X is a hyponym of Y. For example:

Cat is a hyponym of animal.
Chalet is a hyponym of house.
Trilby is a hyponym of hat.
Stiletto is hyponym of shoe.

The reverse relationship is called **hyperonymy**:

Animal is a hypernym of cat.
House is a hypernym of chalet.
Hat is a hypernym of trilby.
Shoe is a hypernym of stiletto.

We can also say that *dog, mouse, horse, pig, lion, cheetah* are *co-hyponyms*. Sometimes the category words such as *animal, house, hat* and *shoe* are referred to as **superordinates**. Their **hyponyms** can be called *subordinates*. Let's look at this graphically in a hyponym tree:

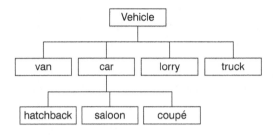

TASK 6

Based on the above hyponym tree, fill in the blanks in the statements below.

a. _____ is a hyponym of *vehicle*.

b. _____ is a hypernym of *lorry*.

c. _____ and _____ are co-hyponyms.

d. _____ is a superordinate of _____.

e. _____, _____ and _____ are subordinates of car.

f. _____ is a superordinate of *coupé*.

Carter (1987) says that hyponymy is a type of asymmetrical synonymy. That is, where two words are related by meaning but the relationship is asymmetrical because one of the words includes the other in its meaning. Hyponymy is very useful in the teaching of new words because co-hyponyms (or subordinates) can be explained in terms of their superordinates. For instance, we can say that a necklace is a type of jewellery. Dictionaries draw on this relationship in their definitions. In the examples of definitions below, we have highlighted the superordinates in bold:

Adjective: *A **word** such as 'small', 'heavy', 'sunny' or 'blue' that describes a person, place or thing or gives extra information about them.*

Bottle: *A **container** for drinks and other liquids usually made of glass or plastic.*

Daffodil: *A yellow spring **flower** which has a bell-shaped centre and a long stem.*

Fanzine: *A **magazine** which is written by fans and is for fans. Usually pop groups and football teams have fanzines.*

Homophones and homographs

Homophones and **homographs** are terms used to refer to relationships between words which are more a matter of coincidence. Neither homophones nor homographs have any semantic relationship.

Homophones are words which have the same pronunciation but are unrelated in meaning. Common examples of *homophones* are:

air – heir	banned – band	cellar – seller	knew – new
aisle – isle	bare – bear	censor – sensor	hair – hare
allowed – aloud	beach – beech	core – corps	hear – here
ate – eight	beat – beet	draft – draught	know – no
bail – bale	ceiling – sealing	dual – duel	leak – leek
bait – bate	cell – sell	fair – fare	mode – mowed

Homographs are words which have the same sign. That is, they look identical but they are unrelated in meaning. Some common homographs are:

	Meaning 1	Meaning 2
bow	/bəʊ/	/baʊ/
	what you use to play the violin	to bend at the waist
lead	/led/	/liːd/
	the heavy metal whose symbol is Pb	to be in front of others
close	/kləʊs/	/kləʊz/
	near to something	to shut something
invalid	/ˋɪnvəlɪd/	/ɪnˋvælɪd/
	a person who is ill	something which is not valid

Usually homographs have different pronunciations. For this reason, they may not cause confusion for learners. What is important from the perspective of teaching words which are homographs is to focus on correct pronunciation.

Metaphor

Lakoff and Johnson (1980) conducted a famous study entitled *Metaphors We Live By*. This showed that metaphor is very common in all forms of language, not just in literature. They illustrate how metaphors are linked to cultural constructions or concepts. Here is an example of how the metaphor of a *fire as a wild beast* is used in a newspaper article. The words used within this metaphor are in bold print:

> Yesterday a fire **broke out** at the Hillsbury Castle owned for generations by the Hampton-Smyth family. It is believed to have begun in the kitchen but very quickly it **got out of control** and **raged** through the whole castle. Eye witnesses say that flames **leaped** high above the roof. Firefighters **fought** the flames for many hours and eventually they were able to **bring it under control**.

TASK 7

Can you think of any example phrases we use for the following metaphors? One example has already been given in each case.

Time as a valuable commodity (That's how I spend my time.)
Love as a journey (Our relationship is on the rocks.)
Argument as war (My point was shot down.)

(Based on Lakoff and Johnson, 1980)

Some of the metaphoric uses of words you may have come up with for *time as a valuable commodity* may have been: *buy time; lose time; waste time; time well spent.* For *love as a journey*, you may have come up with words and phrases such as *we've come a long way together; they went their separate ways; our relationship isn't going anywhere, our relationship is going downhill* or *our relationship is going nowhere; we're going through a rocky patch.* In the case of *argument as war*, you may have listed items such as *He attacked my argument; I demolished his argument; I've never won an argument with him* (based on Lakoff and Johnson, 1980).

Looking at how we use language non-literally, or metaphorically, is very interesting for learners. Very often metaphoric concepts (such as time as a valuable commodity, love as a journey and argument as war) are similar across cultures but sometimes they are not. Metaphoric use of language is pervasive and most texts that we use with our learners contain some degree of non-literal language. This is worth exploring. Metaphor provides a very strong visual connection with meaning and this in turn aids both comprehension and memory. Exploring concordance lines for metaphoric meaning can also be fruitful.

TASK 8

The literal meaning of *die* is not live but it is sometimes used in a non-literal or metaphoric way. Identify which of the following usages are literal and which are non-literal (or metaphoric):

1.	Melissa said she nearly	**died**	when she came out she was
2.	hear one hundred people	**died**	of heat related illnesses in Paris?
3.	street. Gregory Peck. He	**died**.	Who was he? An actor. He was
4.	I'm so sick I'm going to	**die**.	Jealousy gets you no where
5.	four years. I would	**die**.	Actually I nearly died on my twenty
6.	mother. His mother didn't	**die**.	No it was his aunt he's a cousin
7.	a bit of a problem. Did it	**die**?	
8.	is a twin and her mother	**died**	when she was three and her father
9.	I can't wait i'm	**dying**	for it. You are all right do you have
10.	it? Yeah her hamster's	**dying**.	Oh Lord. She's very sick like so

(From the Limerick Corpus of Irish English)

One of the greatest challenges for learners is that there is not always a one-to-one relationship between words. Antonyms and synonyms, while they can be very helpful in understanding the meaning of new words, they can also create problems. As we illustrated in Part A with the words *concur, confab, contradictory* and *contrite* and their synonyms *agree, conversation, opposite* and *sorry* respectively, there are a number of factors which mitigate against a one-to-one relationship. One is register; two words may have the same meaning but they may be used in different registers. If learners are not made aware of register differences, this could generate errors.

Another factor is collocation.

VOCABULARY FILE

Just because words are synonymous does not mean that they share all of the same collocates.

If we look at the collocates of the synonyms *quiet* and *silent* in a corpus, we find very few in common in the first 15 items.

Collocates of *quiet* and *silent* from Collins Corpus Concordance Sample of the Bank of English

quiet	silent
keep	fell
peace	remained
kept	moment
room	long
voice	remain
life	stood
relatively	night
nice	keep
moment	film
shy	majority
keeping	room
man	fall
night	crowd
lanes	kept
street	went

The lack of one-to-one correspondence is also an issue in relation to antonyms. Because of the polysemic nature of words (when words have more than one meaning, see Chapter 2), they often have more than one antonym depending on the meaning or context. Take for example the word *deep*. It has a number of meanings some of which are illustrated in the following sentences. For each meaning, there is a different antonym:

1. *I never swim in the* **deep** *end of the swimming pool.*   (antonym: *shallow*)
2. *Liz is in* **deep** *trouble.*   (antonym: *minor*)
3. *She has a very* **deep** *voice.*   (antonym: *high-pitched*)
4. *Her dress was* **deep** *red velvet.*   (antonym: *bright*)

The challenge for learners is to constantly build up antonyms for all the different meanings of a new word as they encounter them. Also, learning collocational patterns will aid this process. A learner who takes note of the collocational patterns of *deep* (*deep end, deep trouble, deep voice* and *deep red*) is less likely to make mistakes with antonyms in different senses.

Colligation, the grammatical pattern of a word (see Chapter 4), is also a concern in relation to antonymy and synonymy. For example *arrive* and *reach* can be used synonymously to mean 'get to a particular place'. However, their colligational (or grammatical) patterns are not the same:

What time did you **arrive at** *the hotel?* Pattern: *arrive* + at + place
What time did you **reach** *the hotel?* Pattern: *reach* + place

Another major challenge for learners are false cognates (or false friends), which we mentioned in Part A. These are words which look and sound similar or the same in a learner's first language and in English, but which do not have the same meaning. The assumption that they do have the same meaning can lead to transfer errors by learners. There are many common false cognate errors for learners. For example, for Portuguese learners:

English	**Portuguese**
push	*puxar* (means pull)
pretend	*pretender* (means intend)
terrific	*terrivel* (means terrible)

PART C How do we teach it?

The most immediate application of word relations is in the initial presentation of new vocabulary. It would be difficult to explain words without reference to their synonyms, antonym, co-hyponyms, superordinates, and so on.

TASK 9

Write down how you would explain these words to intermediate level students. Then identify the different word relationships which you have used:

tent   plummet

stare   fortnight

As teachers, word relationships seem an obvious way to help us organise the thousands of words that our learners are faced with learning. However, we need to constantly be aware of their limitations. The less we teach words and their synonyms, antonyms and so on in isolation, the more effective sense relations will be.

Especially at more advanced levels, overtly using sense relations in teaching, that is, making students explicitly aware of sense relationships and their terminology, will help in a number of ways. It will create a sense of enquiry when learners encounter new words:

What is its antonym?
Does it have synonyms?
Can its synonyms be used in the same way?
What is the superordinate?
What are the co-hyponyms?

In tandem with this, learners need to build up a critical awareness about these relations. So, they need to be able to ask of a new word and its relations:

Can this synonym be used in the same way?
What other antonyms does this word have and in what contexts?
Is this a true or a false cognate?

Awareness-raising tasks with texts and concordance lines can be of great benefit both in exploring relationships of meaning and in working with non-literal or metaphoric meanings. Here are some possible tasks that you could undertake with your learners using level-appropriate texts or corpora:

1 Use concordance lines of synonyms to explore:
   a. the different senses that each word has
   b. the different collocational patterns that each word has
   c. the different colligational patterns that each word has
   d. how much the two words have in common.

2 Use concordance lines of antonyms to explore:
   a. the different senses that each word has
   b. the different collocational patterns that each word has
   c. the different colligational patterns that each word has
   d. how much the two words have in common.

3 Use concordance lines to explore literal and metaphoric meanings.

4 Select a short level-appropriate text for use as in a reading lesson. As an extension task, ask learners to select three words which they would like to explore further using a dictionary, the Internet or a corpus. Student could report their findings back to the class either orally or in writing. They could address questions such as:

a. What are the synonyms and antonyms of these words?
b. Is this word a superordinate or subordinate?
c. What collocational patterns does each word have?
d. What colligational patterns does each word have?
e. Is this word ever used metaphorically?

5 Build up a class bank of synonyms, antonyms, hyponyms, homophones and homographs. This could be done on cards and posted on the wall or on a shared electronic platform (such as a virtual learning environment). These could be used as the basis for class quizzes where the students test each other. It is important that as much information about collocation and colligation is included as possible.

The important lesson to be learnt about word relations and their application to teaching meaning is 'use with care'. Word relations such as synonymy, antonymy, hyponymy, cognates, and so on, can be a powerful aid to teaching meaning and an aid to memorising new words and sets of words. These relationships can help our learners make connections and help them organise their vocabulary notebooks in a very productive way.

Chapter review

1 What sense relations might you draw on when teaching the following words:

salmon　　　*explore*　　　*dry*　　　*open*　　　*dressing table*

2 Organise the words below into semantic relations and identify the relationship:

bright	bare	scarf
sidewalk	shirt	footpath
dark	bear	rough
smooth	gloves	dress

3 Here is an explanation of a word using its synonym. Give an example of an error which this definition might cause for students.

'To chop means to cut'

4 What are false cognates (or false friends)? Give one example from your own language.

5 We can say that the relationship between *carrot* and *vegetable* is one of hyponymy. What is the reverse relationship called (for example, between *vegetable* and *carrot*)?

6 What is a superordinate?

7 What is the difference between a homophone and a homograph? Give one example of each.

8 Identify the words below which are used metaphorically (or non-literally).

An extract from a report on a football match:

United's game against Liverpool was one nightmare after the other. Their defence were asleep for the entire second half. The forwards threw away numerous chances in front of the goal. With Keane and Rice injured, United's hopes of winning this season are destroyed.

9 Can you think of three different meanings of the word *meet*. For each meaning, give an example and provide a synonym to *meet* in each case.

10 How can concordance lines help us teach meaning?

8 | Words in text and discourse

What is a text?

TASK 1

Look at this simple text produced by a child and answer the questions which follow:

> The little girl cried.
> Her father picked her up.

1   What does 'her' in the second sentence refer to? How do you know?
2   In which order did the events happen? How do we know?
3   Apart from sequence, is there any other possible relationship between the two sentences?
4   What relationship is there between the father and the little girl? How do we know?

This example is based on Sacks (1972) and the questions are based on the discussion in Cameron (2001: 11–12).

Texts have the following properties:

■ They have cohesion – sentences are tied together by cohesive devices.
■ They have coherence – sentences follow each other in ways which make sense.
■ They reflect real-world knowledge – we interpret them by using what we know about what happens in real life.

Texts are the product, but the process by which we make them is called discourse. The study of discourse is discourse analysis, defined by Cameron (2001: 13) as, 'Language in use: language used to do something and mean something, language produced and interpreted in a real-world context'.

Discourse analysis involves studying texts (spoken or written) in naturally occurring contexts such as classrooms, conversations, business meetings (see, for example, Cook, 1989; McCarthy, 1991). By looking at longer stretches of texts, we can learn a lot about their internal structure and organisation. When we look at words in continuous texts, or discourse, we see that they play a key role in creating a sense of order. Words in spoken and written discourse perform important functions which help speakers and writers to establish meanings with their audience.

Lexical cohesion

One feature of both spoken and written discourse is lexical cohesion (Halliday and Hasan 1976). Lexical cohesion refers to the ways in which words give a text a kind of internal unity, a logical structure which helps to create understanding. In casual conversation, for example, we don't simply repeat words, we find alternatives: a synonym, perhaps, or a different way of saying something similar.

Lexis has an important role in creating textuality, as McCarthy (1991: 65) puts it: 'Related vocabulary items occur across clause and sentence boundaries in written texts and across act, move and turn boundaries in speech and are a major characteristic of coherent discourse'. (Turn boundaries occur where one speaker takes over from another.) The main resource for creating textuality through lexical cohesion is reiteration. Reiteration can involve direct repetition of a lexical item, or the exploitation of such lexical relations as synonymy, antonymy and hyponymy (see Chapters 2 and 7).

Consider the following examples:

> When I first got married, I lived in a small terraced house in the middle of the city. It was a modest place, but it was all I needed at that time. A few years later, when the kids came along, we moved to a semi-detached on the outskirts of the town. This spacious property has been our home for more than 20 years, though we're now considering down-sizing to a stone cottage in the country.

Note how cohesion is created across sentence boundaries:

Words for 'house': *terraced house; place; semi-detached; property; stone cottage.*
Expressions of time: *first; at that time; a few years later; for more than 20 years.*
Expressions of place: *city; town; country.*
Words for size: *small; modest; spacious; down-sizing.*

In the above text, the use of related vocabulary items across sentence and clause boundaries creates a sense of internal unity and helps to make the text coherent. Now consider what happens when we 'break the rules' of cohesion in the text below:

> When I first got married, I lived in a small terraced house in the middle of the city. As a bachelor, it was all I needed before that time. The cottage had

a large garden and lots of bedrooms. Although I don't mind living in a small town apartment, my ultimate goal is to move out to a stone cottage in the country.

In this text, there are internal contradictions caused by a lack of lexical cohesion (*married/bachelor; terraced house/cottage/apartment; city/town; small/large garden/ lots of bedrooms*).

TASK 2

Rewrite the text below so that the rules of lexical cohesion are broken:

I was born in Manchester, but spent much of my life moving from one city to another as my father changed jobs frequently. It wasn't surprising then that, after university, I spent many years living in different parts of the world, including Spain, Hong Kong, Hungary and Ireland. I am happy to say that, enjoyable as those times were, I am now back in the UK and happy to stay put – for the time being, at least!

When we look at spoken discourse, we see that speakers choose different words across turn boundaries and rarely repeat each other's exact utterances. Consider these two examples of greetings, the first invented for teaching purposes, the second taken from a genuine interaction:

(1)
A: Hi, how are you?
B: Fine thanks. And you?
A: I'm fine too.
B: Where are you going now?
A: I'm going to visit my friend, Marie.

(2)
A: How ya doing?
B: Good. How are you?
A: Pretty good.
B: What did you think of that film on TV last night? Did you see it?
A: Oh, I loved it. I loved it.

In (1) above, the standard textbook response to 'How are you?' is 'Fine thanks. And you?' The reply 'I'm fine too.' also repeats the greeting. Compare this with (2), a conversation between two friends. Here, Speaker A downtones the response used by Speaker B ('good' to 'pretty good'). Note, too, that Speaker B uses a different question form: 'How are you?' compared with 'How ya doing?' as used by Speaker A. Teachers need to be aware of these differences and exploit them in their teaching; invented examples such as (1) above are best avoided. Extract (2) has greater teaching and learning value in terms of being more natural and more representative of real life.

Lexical chains and topics

TASK 3

In the text below, identify all the examples of lexical choice which contribute to the overall cohesion of the text. Try to classify the different groups of words according to their function and the topic that is under discussion.

> You know, when you hear your parents argue you never understand why they're arguing, you know. Why do they argue? They have three great kids. You know what I mean? And, and then you kind of have to realise that, you know, they're just like any of us, you see. They have lots of problems and they have to deal with it, and it's not so easy to deal with them sometimes, you know.

In this text, it becomes obvious that cohesion is not simply created by pairs of words, as in the previous examples. Here, we have whole chains of vocabulary which contribute to the overall cohesion of this text. They include: *parents; hear; argue; understand; kids; problems; deal with; easy; you know; you know what I mean; kind of.* The topic of the conversation is established and maintained by a conscious selection of related words, 'the vocabulary of a topic' (McCarthy, 1991: 55). These words create main topics and sub-topics, and they help speakers both hold the floor and move from one topic to another.

TASK 4

Consider the short dialogues below. In each one, identify the main topic and circle the words which help to establish and sustain that topic, giving the text cohesion and coherence.

(1)
A: I think I could dance before I sang.
B: Is that so?
A: So I was like four years old.
B: You don't keep it up, do you?
A: Dancing?
B: Yeah.
A: Oh, I can get out there and shake my boogie if I want to.
B: I'll match you any time, OK?
A: OK. Sure.

(2)
A: That would explain why it's stalling. But it should turn on that red warning light, right?
B: Um-hmm.
A: Of course, it may not be working, but we know it works because it goes on when you turn the key on.
B: Right.

Note that the topic words are also content words which carry meaning. In spoken texts, like the two above, it is the content words which are the most prominent in terms of stress. Try reading each one aloud. What do you notice? You should find that the topic words are stressed like this:

A: That would exPLAIN why it's STALLing. But it should TURN ON that RED WARNing LIGHT, RIGHT?
B: UM-hmm.
A: Of COURSE, it may not be WORKing, but we KNOW it WORKS because it GOES ON when you turn the KEY ON.
B: RIGHT.

VOCABULARY FILE

Once we understand that (a) cohesion is created by key words in a text and (b) those key words receive greater prominence (that is, they are stressed), we can really help learners become much more fluent in both speaking and writing.

When we consider how topics are created and sustained in language classrooms, the picture is even more complicated owing to the rapid to-and-fro of the discourse, the many participants and the rapid topic changes. Sustaining cohesion in the class-room requires considerable interactional agility on the part of the teacher. When topics are switched too quickly or when they are not marked in some way, learners become confused and get lost in the discourse (Breen, 1998).

TASK 5

Consider the extract below, taken from a multilingual ESL classroom with adult, pre-intermediate learners. The topic under discussion is 'pot-luck suppers'.

Identify the vocabulary items which help to create and sustain the topic.
Where is the topic 'switched' and what is the effect on the discourse?
How might the teacher have marked this topic shift more clearly?

45 T: Oh dear, well, Georgia, perhaps when you go back to Italy, perhaps you can organise one of these typical pot-luck suppers, and organise it well so you'll have plenty of desserts and plenty of starters, but do you think it's a good idea?
46 L: Sometimes, yeah
47 L: It's nice because you don't know what you're going to eat
48 T: It's a surprise yes, yeah as long as you like everything … I mean some people don't like certain things. What adjective do we use for people who don't like that and hate that, and a lot of food they won't eat … we call it people are very … FUSsy fussy with their food (writes on BB), right? So, fussy, that's don't like vegetables, never eat pasta …
49 L1: Excuse me, how to say if you, for example, if you try some burger on corner … on the the street and then you feel not very well
50 T Er … I'm not quite sure what you mean, Yvette, if you …?
51 L1: You can buy, for example, just on the street
52 T: You mean street sellers … people selling food on the street, yes?

Stance

When words appear in a written or spoken text, they may show the speaker's or writer's attitude or position towards something. This is especially common in academic writing, where writers normally adopt a particular stance in relation to a subject, expressing agreement, disagreement, confirmation and so on. In order to do this, writers use certain lexical signals (McCarthy, 1991) to show the reader how key elements of a text are organised and how they relate to one another. These signals give a text direction and let the reader know what's coming next, what's already been mentioned, and so on. Compare Extracts 3 and 4 below, both taken from a corpus of student writing. Extract 3 is an example of effective writing; the underlined words show how the writer has taken a particular position and indicate both the 'what' and the 'how' of the proposed study. Some of the more abstract words (such as *principal aim, a range of data, desired outcome, improvement of practice, a distinct relation, in the field of*) signal relations to the reader and help to give the text its internal cohesion and overall coherence. Note, too, how many of these words are collocations (*principal aim, statistically analyse, obvious improvement*, and so on): words which combine naturally together (see Chapter 3). Collocation is another device which adds to the lexical cohesion of a text.

(3)

This dissertation involves a <u>small-scale</u>, <u>empirical study</u>. The <u>principal aim</u> is to statistically analyse a range of data based on surveys, student and teacher interviews and classroom observation. The <u>desired outcome</u> is an obvious improvement of practice within the learning behaviour of the students. The paper is set in a theoretical context with a <u>distinct relation</u> to research literature <u>in the field of</u> training vocabulary learning strategies.

Now consider Extract 4. This text is more awkward and causes some reader strain, partly because there is less signalling and more repetitions of words (*subject*), misuses of groups of words such as *carry out the target language, organise the structure*, and inaccuracies such as *takes into account of.*

(4)

A textbook usually consists of detailed information about the <u>subject</u> for learners who are studying the specific subject. It not only enriches <u>the quality of the language classroom</u> but also provides clear structures to learners, so that the students have a holistic view of the lessons. At the same time, it helps language teachers <u>to carry out the target language</u> (Nunan, 2003). Also, teachers can <u>organise the structure</u> of the language courses. As a result, using a textbook not only <u>takes into account of</u> students' needs as second language learners, but also facilitates the learners' learning processes (Cunningsworth, 1995).

(McCarthy et al., 2007)

TASK 6

Rewrite Extract 4 in such a way that the text's overall cohesion is improved. Make use of key lexical signals to help show how the text is organised. Underline these and then consider what alternatives might have been used.

Register

You will remember that we spoke about register and connotation in Chapter 2, and it is also important here. When we consider words in text (spoken and written), it becomes very clear that the actual choice of words is not random, that both speakers and listeners select their words according to who they are communicating with, as well as why, where, how and when. The relationship between these features is called register. Halliday's (1978) model identifies the features of contexts in which language is being used, the key ones being:

- field, which relates to the subject and purpose of the message (for example, a newspaper advertisement for a job)
- tenor, which denotes the relationship between the sender and receiver (for example, two colleagues or a husband and wife)
- mode, that is, how the message is communicated (conversation, telephone, and so on).

In practical terms, what this means is that we don't (and can't) simply select words at random. Depending on who we are talking/writing to, why we are talking/writing, how we are talking/writing, and so on, we must use a vocabulary which is 'context sensitive'. Typically, this will involve selecting words which are more or less formal, according to the situation. For example, how would you respond to the question: *How was your week end?* when asked by:

- your boss
- a friend
- a member of your family
- someone you have just met?

In each case, your selection of words would depend on how formal/informal the relationship is between you and each interlocutor and, also, how much shared knowledge you have (Cook, 1989). Our interactions with others in both spoken and written texts are largely based on principles of cooperation and politeness (Grice, 1975; Watts, 2003).

TASK 7

For each of the following short texts, provide a context and say what type of text it is. Which key words in the text helped you to identify these features?

1. Enriched with soothing cucumber and vitamins, this gentle moisturiser works to hydrate skin while UV filters and antioxidants help protect the skin from environmental damage.
2. Please note that this facility is offered to allow you to pay your service charge in full. If you wish to pay monthly then a direct debit payment facility is available.
3. Weather great, hotel awful, food even worse! Wish you were here – or I was there!
4. I have booked the Howden for 12–5 (just to cover all options) on 11th December (absolutely nothing available in KRC). But just to complicate issues further, Frank can't do the 11th!

PART B What are the problems for learners?

For learners, words in continuous spoken or written English pose a number of problems. For example, the form of a word may change when it is used in different contexts (*giant* and *gigantic*, for example), meanings are often highly context-specific and change from one context to another; even the pronunciation of a word changes when it appears in continuous speech. When we consider the problems that learners face when dealing with words in texts, it is useful to consider each of the four skills in turn.

Listening

According to Ur (1996), listening in real life has some of the following characteristics:

- Much spoken language is informal, unplanned and spontaneous.
- Pronunciation is not always distinct – word boundaries are 'slurred'.
- Informal speech makes use of a lot of slang and idiomatic language.
- Ungrammatical utterances occur frequently.
- Background 'noise' causes interference.
- High levels of redundancy are common.
- Receivers only get 'one chance' as speakers usually only say something once.
- Listeners nearly always know something about the topic. There is a degree of shared knowledge which allows listeners to have expectations
- People usually have a reason to listen – there is nearly always a listening *purpose*.
- Visual clues are used a lot to process incoming language.
- Listeners respond to what they hear.
- Speech is directed and *tailored* to listener.

It is clear that, for most learners, even the most advanced ones, listening poses a significant challenge. The incoming stream of speech is often fast, accented, uses a lot of local vernacular or slang, contains false starts, rephrasing and elaborations, and may contain many non-grammatical forms of words. Consider the following list of comments made by learners:

I have trouble catching the sounds of the language.

I find I need to understand every word, otherwise I feel I am not catching everything that is said to me.

I cannot understand fast speech – people here speak too quickly for me!

I don't understand the local accent.

I need to hear things more than once to understand.

I get tired after a while and cannot concentrate on what is being said.

Telephone conversations are the most difficult thing for me.

Sometimes the topic is too 'culturally loaded' for me and I cannot understand.

Reading

Reading and listening are often considered 'passive' skills in that there is no real production of language. In fact, both are very active and require considerable processing skills by learners. While some of the difficulties experienced by learners when listening to a 'text' are similar to the ones outlined above in relation to listening, reading poses other challenges. Here are some of the more common ones experienced by learners:

- They try and understand every word.
- They cannot read quickly enough.
- They get 'lost' in a text.
- *Lexical density* is too high.
- *Cultural content* is unknown to them.
- Topic familiarity is a problem.
- They have no interest in the topic of the text.

Typically, many learners employ poor reading strategies because they have never been taught how to read in English and may import 'bad' habits from reading in their own language. A recurring problem among learners at all levels is the feeling that they have to understand every word in a text to fully understand it. Part of the role of the teacher is to help learners develop strategies which will allow them to ignore non-essential vocabulary, while paying closer attention to the key words of a text. We'll return to this in Part C below.

Speaking

According to Bygate (1988), it is only when learners are speaking that they have an opportunity to work out what they want to say and therefore acquire new language. Speaking presents many difficulties for learners in terms of vocabulary use. Many speaking tests, such as IELTS, measure the ability of candidates to make flexible use of vocabulary. This may not mean always being able to use the right word in a given context, but having strategies which enable a learner to circumlocute (literally find their way around) a word and use an alternative.

In rapid, fluent, conversational speech, one of the most important skills a speaker has to master is the ability to make a timely contribution. This in turn is dependent on the speaker being able to retrieve a word from memory. Lewis (2002) talks about the 'Mental Lexicon' and describes the ways in which words are organised in our minds so that retrieval is easy (see also Chapter 9 in this book). For example, retrieval is helped by contextual clues, our ability to match spoken input to stored sounds and spellings and the use of anchor words – words which tend to have 'fixed' meanings. Retrieval is also dependent on learners' ability to produce lexical chunks rather than focusing on individual words.

VOCABULARY FILE

According to McCarthy (1995), the retrieval of words is related to the 'bathtub effect' – we can often say something about the beginning and end of a word, but little about the middle, which 'dips'.

It is clear now that learners need to know more in to produce a word than they do in order to recognise it. So, for speaking, learners require greater lexical knowledge than they do for reading, for example. Some practitioners suggest that, for this reason, we should focus more on receptive skills like reading and listening and allow learners time before asking them to speak or write.

In the extract below, the teacher (T) works quite hard to help the learner (L5) find the right words to express her exact meaning. There is considerable negotiation of meaning (in 130, 132 and 134) where the teacher tries to help the learner find the precise phrase she is looking for. Finally, the teacher rephrases the learner's phrase 'do many different experiences' (137) and gives her the phrase 'believe in experiencing as many different things as you want' (138). This extract shows quite clearly how learners often struggle when trying to express themselves orally. It also shows the key role that teachers play in negotiation meanings and in scaffolding a turn. Here, the teacher provides the language the learner needs in 138.

129	L5:	I believe in trying new things and ideas
130	T:	Er, you believe in being POSitive you mean?
131	L5:	Pardon?
132	T:	Do you believe in always being positive? Is that what you mean?
133	L5:	No ... I believe to, to have a lot of achievement
134	T:	Do you believe in – what do you mean – you should always take opportunities, is that what you mean, no?
135	L5:	No, I want my life to be very
136	T:	Happy?
137	L5:	Yeah and also I do many things, many different experiences
138	T:	Why don't you say you just believe in experiencing as many different things as you want?
139	L5:	Oh, yeah
140.	T:	That's what I think you should say

Writing

Writing presents its own problems in terms of vocabulary use. Not only do learners have to find the right word to express themselves, they must also get the grammar right (by using the correct form of a word), use correct spelling, and select a word which is appropriate to the *genre*. For example, an informal letter will require a different selection of vocabulary to a covering letter for a job interview. Many learners tend to 'genre switch' in their writing, moving from formal to informal in academic writing, for example, or using language which is overly formal.

When we look at student writing, even using a small corpus of student academic writing, it is possible to detect common problems, which might include things such as:

- an under- or over-use of discourse markers: *first, in addition, however*, and so on
- a lack of attention to cohesion and coherence.
- a failure to use an adequate range of vocabulary
- little attention given to the audience

TASK 9

Look at the extract below, taken from the *Learner Corpus of Dissertation Writing* (LCDW, Walsh, 2007). This extract comes from the first 100 words of a dissertation. What does it tell us about this student's writing? What vocabulary difficulties can you identify? How would you deal with them if this was one of your students?

This introduction explores the traditional English language teaching (ELT) in universities in China and the new approaches to teaching English using computer-assisted software in recent years, followed by briefly discussion of the structure of this dissertation. The purpose of this study is to examine the effect of information technology as a media for teach language in improving Chinese learners' spoken English and their motivating.

PART C How do we teach it?

Teaching words in texts involves giving learners appropriate strategies so that they can both *process* and *produce* new language. In reading and listening texts, students will be faced with many new words, some essential to their understanding, some useful and some which can be ignored. One way of helping learners is to get them to mark all the unknown words in a text and then mark them again according to whether they are necessary (N) or not necessary (NN) for understanding. Another is to get learners used to asking 'ghost questions' (questions inside learners' heads which help make sense of a text). These questions will relate to both the linguistic and world knowledge features of a text. Some writers suggest that getting learners to 'think aloud' as they try to guess the meanings of new words is also a useful teaching strategy (see Oxford, 1990).

Getting learners to identify the lexical relations in a text is also a very useful way of both helping them to develop comprehension skills and the skills needed to write in a cohesive and coherent way. Colour-coding a text can be very helpful: learners use a different colour to circle each member of a lexical set. Take the following text, for example.

> When I travel abroad, I am always careful to make sure that I have planned the entire trip from start to finish so that I can be confident that I haven't forgotten anything. Although this works most of the time, I was on a recent trip to America when my luggage went missing. It was three days before it eventually arrived, by which time I'd bought an entire new wardrobe and set of toiletries. No amount of careful planning could have helped me to predict that.

You could use a different colour to circle these lexical sets:

- Travel words: travel, abroad, America, trip, luggage, wardrobe, toiletries.
- Time expressions: from start to finish, most of the time, recent, three days, eventually, by which time.
- Words related to 'care': careful, make sure, confident.
- Plans: planned, forgotten, planning, predict.

Another skill which learners need to develop when dealing with words in texts is inference, or reading/listening 'between the lines'. Inferring involves constructing meanings by using a combination of linguistic and world knowledge. For example, in the text above about travel, let's imagine that a learner didn't know the word *trip*. In order to work out the meaning of that word, learners have a number of resources to help them infer meaning:

- Lexical knowledge: trip must be a noun as it is preceded by articles and adjectives (entire, recent).
- Knowledge of co-text (words immediately surrounding *trip*): here, *planned* and *America* are useful clues in inferring the meaning from co-text. A trip is something that you plan and go on.
- World knowledge: learners bring their knowledge of the world and their own personal experience to a text. In this case, learners' knowledge and experience of travel would help them to infer the meaning of *trip*.

Note that while teachers often *tell* learners to infer meanings from a text, they rarely *teach* this skill as explicitly as we have demonstrated here.

VOCABULARY FILE

> It is definitely worth spending some time teaching inference as learners will benefit hugely from developing their own strategies.

Apart from guessing and inferring meanings in both listening and reading texts, learners should be taught how to *predict* meanings. One way of doing this is to use nonsense words in a text.

Read the text below and write down what you think the nonsense words mean. Then analyse how you did it; make a list of the strategies you used to make sense of the unknown words.

Holiday travellers faced long GRINTS today as French air traffic PLONIANS went on strike for the third day in FRENTLION. At this busy time of year, the resulting effect was SHRIDIC. Many flights were delayed by up to six hours and some were even GANNELLED. Travellers were left WRADED at airports and many were unable to leave owing to security regulations.

Getting learners to produce their own texts and nonsense words and exchange them is enormously motivating and great fun! It can be used both to help develop vocabulary skills and also to help with reading and writing.

One classroom activity which is extremely helpful in getting learners to acquire vocabulary is a *dictogloss*. This is a kind of interactive dictation in which learners have to first listen to a text and then re-produce what they've heard. Close attention to words and their associated meanings is necessary in order to complete the task satisfactorily. Typically, the following procedure is used:

1 Select a short text (100–150 words).

2 Read the text aloud, students make notes from what they hear.

3 Working in pairs, students compare notes and make sure they have recorded all the key details.

4 Read the text a second time, students check their notes and add, amend, and so on.

5 Again, working in pairs, students re-write the text in their own words and using their notes.

6 Read the text a third time. Students check their version of the text and amend as necessary.

7 Give the original text to students so that they can compare it with their own version.

The main advantage of a dictogloss is that it offers an integrated approach to training skills. Listening, reading, speaking and writing are all practised. It also entails a considerable amount of negotiation of meaning of new vocabulary as students discuss and then attempt to reproduce the text. Texts should be relatively simple, humorous if possible and contain some (but not too many) new vocabulary items. For more ideas on using dictogloss, see Wajnryb (1990).

In this chapter we have looked at the ways in which texts are created and how words play a key function in creating and maintaining texts. When we look at words in context in continuous texts (called **discourse**), we see how they play a key role in creating a sense of order. Words in spoken and written discourse perform important functions which help speakers and writers to establish meanings with their audience. Lexical cohesion is one aspect of this sense of order – it refers to the ways in which words give a text a kind of internal unity. In addition, the relationships between words help to establish topics and sub-topics and help speakers move from one topic to another. In written texts, a writer's choice of whole strings of words helps to establish a particular relationship with the audience and allows the writer to adopt a particular position or stance in relation to a topic. In short, we have seen that both speakers and writers make conscious and deliberate choices of vocabulary, which they combine in texts to ensure maximum communicative impact. By promoting an understanding how words operate in texts, we can help learners to communicate more effectively.

Chapter review

1 What are the key features of texts?

2 What do we mean by lexical cohesion and why is it important?

3 In the short text below, circle the words which help to give the text its internal cohesion.

To what extent do teachers of EFL hinder or facilitate learner contributions by their use of language? How can teachers enhance the quantity and quality of learner output by more careful language use? In what ways do teachers deny learning opportunities by 'filling in the gaps' or 'smoothing over' learner contributions? Adopting the position that maximising learner involvement is conducive to second language acquisition, this paper examines the ways in which teachers, through their choice of language, construct or obstruct learner participation in face to face classroom communication.

(Walsh, 2002)

4 How are lexical signals used to give cohesion to a text?

5 Explain what Halliday means by *field, tenor* and *mode*. How might this help in the teaching of vocabulary?

6 Why might the *lexical density* of a text be a problem for learners? How can we deal with it?

7 Explain what is meant by inference. Why do we need to teach it?

8 What types of knowledge do we typically use to make sense of a text?

9 Write a short text of around 50–60 words. Include 6–8 nonsense words. What knowledge about words in texts did you use to 'create' these nonsense words?

10 Devise one activity designed to help learners understand cohesion.

9 | Words in the mind

How the mind organises vocabulary

In our native language (L1), we are able to store, retrieve and use vast quantities of words. Educated adult speakers use tens of thousands of words, usually quickly and easily. How can we explain this phenomenon? How do we store so many words and retrieve them so quickly? What processes are at work and are they same in L1 and L2 (second language)?

Any discussion which looks at words in the mind, or our **mental lexicon,** is based on partial understandings. After all, the mind is not a machine that we can easily open up to see how it works! However, we can use our observations of how language is used, and how we behave with language, as a means of understanding how words are stored and retrieved. We can use different metaphors to help further these understandings, such as a dictionary, an encyclopaedia, a thesaurus, a computer and so on.

If we use the computer analogy, we can see that very much depends on memory size and processor speed. But it also depends on the ways in which we input, store and retrieve data. There are strong correlations between the ways in which a computer works and the ways in which our mental lexicon works. However, we should not assume that the processes are the same in L1 and L2. We'll come back to this later in the chapter.

VOCABULARY FILE

Based on what we know so far about words in the mind, we can say that:

- Words appear to be organised in some way in our minds.
- There is far more to knowing a word than knowing its form and meaning.
- Knowledge of vocabulary is linked very closely with our knowledge of the world.
- Input, storage and retrieval of words are important processes which need to be understood.
- Words have a *general shape* which gives us vital clues about their form, meaning and use.

Let's now look at the various processes that determine the ways in which words are organised in the mind:

- Input: the ways in which we record words.
- Storage: the ways in which we retain words.
- Retrieval: the ways in which we recall words.

Input

TASK 1

What are the main differences between learning vocabulary in an L1 and learning vocabulary in an L2? Complete the table below.

	L1	L2
1.		
2.		
3.		
4.		
5.		

Some of the differences are immediately obvious. For example, when we learn our first language, we are babies with very little knowledge of the world. Most people learn their second language when they are older, with considerable experience of the world. Some would say that learning vocabulary in the L2 simply involves 'relabelling the world', although it is unlikely to be so simple.

The input L2 learners receive is clearly very different. Whereas babies only receive spoken input, most L2 learners receive both spoken and written input. In fact, in many parts of the world, they receive more written than spoken input. The implication is that learners are exposed to rules about both spelling (orthography) and sounds (phonology) from a very early stage. Learners are often able to recall the basic sound or spelling of a word: 'it sounds like x', 'it begins with 's'.

Words have a *general shape* which gives us vital clues about their form, meaning and use. (You may remember the 'bathtub effect' from Chapter 8, the idea of someone lying in a bath of water with only their head and feet visible at either end.)

- The bathtub effect: We can often say something about the beginning and end of a word, but little about the middle which 'dips' (Aitchison, 1976).
- Tip of the tongue phenomenon: We may have a word 'on the tip of our tongue' and be able to say quite a lot about it without recalling the exact word.

TASK 2

How many words can you think of which have these 'bathtub' patterns?

- im------ly
- pro-----ion
- un------ly
- d-----ion
- i------able

From a teaching point of view, the implications are that much important information comes at the beginning and end of a word. Learners need to be made aware of this and use specific strategies to store new words (see Part C of this chapter). Teachers also need to be aware of the amount and type of input that learners need. Much research about second language acquisition has focused on input (and **output**, see Part B below).

According to Krashen and Terrell (1983), second language acquisition works best when learners are exposed to comprehensible input, or input which is at, or slightly above, the learners' current level of proficiency ($i + 1$). Of course, while this is a very useful ideal, in practice, most learners have different levels of language proficiency; what is $i + 1$ for one learner may be $i + 25$ for another. Nonetheless, Krashen does raise a very important point in terms of the need for teachers to grade new language to the level of the group they are teaching. One way of grading language is to consider the lexical variation of a text, that is, how many new words does it have in relation to known ones? Some researchers (see, for example, McCarthy, 1990) suggest that learners can handle one new word per every 15 in a text, a total of around 50 words in a text of 750 words. Of course, this is a guide only and other factors (such as topic familiarity, occurrences of technical words and jargon, and so on) would have to be taken into account.

TASK 3

How many words in the text below are unknown to you? How did you deal with them?

The two centre AO expansion, introduced by Bates and McCaroll (1958) centres a travelling atomic basis around each nucleus and has produced accurate cross sections for electron capture at velocities close to the Bohr velocity. The model was improved by the inclusion of pseudostates, which accurately represent the dominant bound states, along with truncation of the complete set of basis functions, where the continuum states are accurately represented. However, as mentioned earlier, the Atomic Orbital (AO) expansion does not accurately represent the molecular nature of the interaction during close collisions. Two closely related approaches have been developed to correct this by accurately representing the electronic distribution during these close collisions.

(Thompson, 1995)

Storage

If words are to be retrieved and stored easily, we presumably have a considerable amount of information about words to facilitate the retrieval process. Using the analogy of a dictionary entry, we can learn the following about any one word:

- its spelling
- its pronunciation
- its word class
- its meaning
- its derivations
- references to synonyms and collocations
- its register and any connotations.

For many learners, spelling is the first point of reference when trying to recall a word from storage. This might be due to the fact that, for most of us, learning a second language takes place in school where there is a heavy emphasis on the written word. We are able to recall many words which have similar spellings.

TASK 4

See how quickly you can call up other English words with similar spellings to these words. Find three more examples for each one and time yourself!

| pail | sale | comb | loan | phone |

While it is beneficial for learners to make use of this kind of knowledge, there is now considerable evidence that words are not stored in isolation – nor according to spellings – but in association with other words. We have already seen in Chapter 7 how useful it can be to think of words in terms of their *semantic relationships*, or **semantic networks**, comprising related words. One useful way of storing words is to get learners to collect vocabulary items in families or networks. Here's an example for *politics*:

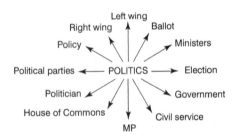

It does seem, then, that we store words in large bundles which are inter-linked and which have relations with other words. The metaphor of a thesaurus is useful here because a thesaurus organises words according to their semantic relations with other words.

Most of the evidence so far suggests that the storage and retrieval of words in the mind is heavily influenced by words' semantic relations. For example, if I think of the word *grass*, my first association is with its colour *green*. If I think of the word *black*, *white* is the word which comes to mind. In the first example, the association is by **collocation** (*green grass*), which you may remember from Chapters 3 and 7, while in the second, it is by **antonymy** (*black* is the opposite of *white*), which you may remember from Chapters 2 and 7. Other types of association, which we have already looked at, include:

Synonymy: where a word with a similar meaning is given (see Chapter 2 and Chapter 7).
Superordination: where a superordinate is given (e.g. *vehicle* is the superordinate of *lorry*; *lorry* belongs to the class which we know as *vehicle*; see Chapter 7.)

TASK 5

For each of the following words, write down one association, the first word which comes to your mind. Try to explain which process of association you used (collocation, synonymy, antonymy, superordination):

   cat   January   impossible   table   bad-tempered

We have seen how semantic relations between words are important for storage. But this doesn't tell the whole story. Words have meanings for us in other, more personal ways. For example, if I were to draw a network for *holidays*, I would come up with something like this, based on my own experiences and knowledge of the world:

The kind of knowledge of a word that is represented here is clearly quite different to that presented in a dictionary. In this case, knowing a word brings together linguistic, experiential and world knowledge. It suggests that our storage of words is closely related to the ways in which we store memories and experiences. Rather than thinking of words as stored in the mind in neat and tidy 'filing cabinets', this view of storage suggests that we should think in terms of webs or networks. It is the relationship or association between words which is important here. Note, too, how this perspective recognises that each web – each network – is constantly updated as new vocabulary is acquired. The metaphor of a web or network which is constantly in a state of flux is, perhaps, the most useful one since it conveys the dynamic nature of the mental lexicon, the fact that it is never actually 'finished'. Connections in the brain between words are constantly made and re-made, strengthened and solidified. This theory of how words are stored is often referred to as **connectionism** (Ellis, 1997).

Retrieval

What does it really mean when we say we 'know' a word? One of the features of knowing a word is being able to summon it as and when it is needed.

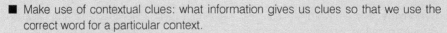

Retrieval depends on our ability to:

- Make use of contextual clues: what information gives us clues so that we use the correct word for a particular context.

- Match spoken or written input to stored sounds and spellings: this means that learners must be able to relate what they see or hear to what they have stored and then recall an appropriate word to formulate a response.

- Use **anchor words**, words which tend to have 'fixed' meanings (see Chapter 8).

- Decode 'chunks' of language, but also recognise individual meanings, for example, *by and large* (see Chapter 5).

It is clear that learners need to be able to retrieve words at the very moment in time that they are needed. It is also true to say that retrieval differs according to whether it is **receptive** or **productive.** According to McCarthy (1990: 43), receptive retrieval 'involves matching spoken or written input to stored sound and orthographic patterns and their associated meanings'. This is why, for example, in a reading activity, it is important to get learners NOT to focus on every individual word, but to simply *recognise* words. In this way, they will become both faster and more efficient.

Productive retrieval means being able to make more active use of a word, in a piece of writing, for example. Note that receptive and productive here should not be equated with active and passive, terms sometimes reserved for talking about the four skills and the idea that 'reading is passive, speaking is active'. Receptive and productive retrieval simply highlight the fact that we do not use words in the same way all the time. For example, when scanning a newspaper for some piece of information, receptive retrieval may be adequate, whereas writing an academic essay requires a more active retrieval of words.

TASK 6

Use the prompts below to retrieve the five missing words. What clues did you use?

to modernise or regenerate a town, city or residential area (g_____)

a tool used for removing nails, etc. (p_____)

to disappear forever (b_____ e_____)

a musical instrument, a little like a guitar (b_____)

part of a bicycle, used to change gears (d_____)

In a classroom, the teacher plays a significant role in helping learners to retrieve vocabulary items. A considerable amount of research has been done on **word searches** in recent years, in other words, the strategies used by learners to retrieve vocabulary as and when needed (see for example, Ellis, 1994). In the extract below, note how the learner shows that she is searching for a word (20–22). The teacher feeds in (also known as scaffolding, which you may remember from Chapter 8) the missing word in 23 and this is repeated as a confirmation in 24, together with a gesture in 25–26.

20   Farah: Your, uh, your body can not put in the, your family

21   [draws a square in

22		the air]
23	T:	Tomb
24	Farah:	Ya, family tomb
25		[Nodding and draw the same square in the air again]
26	T:	Okay

(Fen-Lan Lin, 2009)

For this exchange to be successful, teachers must first of all recognise that a learner is trying to retrieve a word, provide appropriate input and then check that the learner has understood. Considerable interactional agility is needed on the teacher's part in order to help the learner retrieve a word.

In the example below, notice how the teacher *guides* the class through a combination of questions and prompts to the word he is trying elicit. Note that learners already know the word; the teacher is simply trying to help one learner retrieve it in a specific context:

187	T:	What do we call, I'm going to try and get the class to tell you what this word is that you're looking for … er, we talk about military [claps hands] … military what?
188.	L:	[undecipherable]
189	T:	Like fight
190	L:	Kill
191	T:	No, not kill
192	L:	Action, action
193	T:	Military?
194	LL:	Power
195	T:	Power. Think of another word … military?
196	LL:	Force
197	T:	So, she believes in a FORCE for?
198	L:	That guide our lives.
199	T:	That guides our lives.

Here, the teacher uses a combination of **direct repair** (in 191), and questions to help learners retrieve the word 'force' (in 196). Direct repair involves correcting an error quickly and simply without interrupting the flow of the discourse. His strategy alerts learners to the collocation 'military force', which they clearly knew already, but which needed appropriate prompts to get them to produce it.

PART B What are the problems for learners?

In Part A, we already touched on some of the main problems that learners face. They relate to:

Input: What do learners *do* with the new words which they are exposed to?
Storage: How do learners *record* new vocabulary (both in writing in their minds)?
Retrieval: How do learners *recall* vocabulary at a time when it is needed?

Most vocabulary acquisition is implicit, or 'accidental'. While teachers often adopt certain classroom procedures and techniques to make vocabulary acquisition more explicit, it is fair to say that learners acquire most of their new words implicitly, or unconsciously.

The implications of this body of research are that some approaches (or **learning strategies**) to learning vocabulary are more effective than others and learners need to be made aware of this. Learning strategies refer to the deliberate actions that learners take to help them acquire new language (see, for example, Oxford, 1990). Examples include: watching films in the L2, keeping an index file of new vocabulary, recording new words on an voice-recording device, and so on. More specifically, learning strategies for vocabulary can range from straightforward measures like using flash-cards or finding direct translations, to more cognitively demanding strategies such as interacting with peers and teachers and seeking out semantically related words (Schmitt, 1997; see also Chapter 10).

TASK 7

Which of the following vocabulary learning strategies are effective (E) and which are ineffective (I). How did you decide?

a Reciting vocabulary from a dictionary _____

b Writing vocabulary lists in both English and the L1 equivalent _____

c Recording new words according to their 'word family', possibly as a semantic network (see above) _____

d Writing to a pen pal _____

e Underlining every new word in a text and checking its meaning in a dictionary

_____

f Watching films which are subtitled in English _____

g Reading extensively in English _____

h Listening to the radio in English _____

Clearly, different strategies are more or less appropriate according to the level of the group which is being taught. At beginner or low-intermediate levels, learners may struggle with the sheer volume of new words they have to deal with. Here, rote-learning and translation into L1 may be entirely appropriate. At more advanced levels, learners need to become more independent and develop appropriate metacognitive strategies for dealing with new words, such as guessing meaning from context, inferring and using world knowledge and contextual clues to predict the meanings of new words.

Other problems which learners encounter are related to our earlier discussion on what it means to 'know' a word. Knowing a word involves knowing:

- Its spelling: learners may have difficulty spelling certain words.

- Its pronunciation: words may be difficult to pronounce for a number of reasons, including the lack of a one-to-one relationship between sound and spelling, unusual stress patterns, and so on.

- Its form: learners frequently choose the wrong form of a word (they say *interesting* when they mean *interested*, for example).

- Its meaning: words with similar meanings create huge problems for learners.

- Its derivations: it is easy to trace the roots of some words, while others create more difficulties (see 'false friends' in Chapter 7).
- Collocations: knowing how words combine with other words is central to learning new vocabulary (see Chapter 3).
- Its connotations and register (see Chapter 10).

What is apparent is that learners may not know all words to the same degree, as we have just discussed. We should evaluate any difficulties our learners encounter in terms of what level of knowledge they need to have of a particular word.

PART C How do we teach it?

Approaches to teaching vocabulary are heavily influenced by theories of **second language acquisition** (SLA) which attempt to explain how languages are learnt. We will now look briefly at some of the more salient theories in terms of vocabulary acquisition and summarise the implications of each one for teaching and learning.

Behaviourism

Under **behaviourism** (see Skinner, 1953), vocabulary learning (and, indeed, any aspect of language learning) is treated as a process of habit formation, like learning to use chopsticks, or a knife and fork, or ride a bicycle. The emphasis is on imitation, repetition and reinforcement, and habits are simply 'transferred' from L1 to L2. While rote-learning of vocabulary is certainly not adequate for language acquisition to take place, it is still practised in many parts of the world. It may, as we saw earlier, be entirely appropriate at the early stages of learning a second language, but it is unlikely to work at more advanced levels as learners will become bored and frustrated by a perceived lack of progress. There is evidence that, as learners become more advanced, they enjoy and benefit from more cognitively engaging strategies for learning vocabulary (Schmitt, 1997).

Note in the extract below how the teacher listens to each learner contribution and reinforces each one by first repeating it and then writing it on the board. This process of listen, model and write is very effective at lower levels (this is a pre-intermediate class), but would seem out of place with higher levels.

L: Break, break, breakfast
T: Breakfast [writes on board]
L: Curry
T: Curry [writes on board]
L: Bland
T: Bland [writes on board]
(Walsh, 2001)

TASK 8

Evaluate the appropriacy of behaviourism: to what extent can learning vocabulary be considered as a process of habit formation?

Cognitivism

In direct contrast to behaviourism, **cognitivist** theories of SLA maintain that language acquisition is a cognitive activity. The best known name in this tradition is Chomsky, whose theory of Universal Grammar (1965) argues that we all have an innate ability to learn a language during a critical period of our lives, normally by the age of about ten. He maintains that we, as human beings are pre-disposed to language acquisition. In terms of input, proponents of this tradition argue that input should be at or slightly above the learners' current level (see Krashen, i+1, discussed earlier). They also say that there should be a **silent period** when learners are not expected to say anything.

In terms of teaching vocabulary, this theory approximates to what we have seen above under a strong-implicit view of learning new words. New words are simply acquired unconsciously; no amount of teaching will influence this process of acquisition and learners should simply be left to 'get on with it'.

Interactionist theories of SLA

Proponents of this theory of learning suggest that learning takes place through the interaction which occurs between teacher and learners, and learners and other learners. Advanced initially by Long (1983, 1996), the theory holds that learning takes place when meanings are negotiated. The **negotiation of meaning** is therefore central to any learning task, including vocabulary acquisition. In terms of teaching new vocabulary, learning is maximised when learners are working with each other and when they are seeking clarification, checking meaning and making sure that understandings occur. We will return to this theme of interacting in Chapter 10.

In the extract below, we can see how meanings are being negotiated around some new vocabulary. In 1, learner 1's contribution discographics sparks off a surprised reaction from the teacher who seeks clarification in 2. This prompts a fairly lengthy explanation in 3, followed by some modification and scaffolding in 4 by the teacher, who introduces the new vocabulary: 'music business'. This is then fine-tuned in 5 and 6 where both L1 and the teacher come to a negotiated agreement: 'music industry'.

The give and take of the interaction in this extract illustrates very well how new meanings are not simply 'delivered'; they are negotiated through classroom talk, by confirmation checks and requests for clarification.

1. L1: Discographics
2. T: Ooh, what do you mean?
3. L1: The people who, not the people, the, the business about music record series and
4. T: Is this a word you're thinking of in Basque or Spanish? In English I don't know this word 'disco-graphics' what I would say is, er [writes on board] like you said, 'the music business'
5. L1: The music business? What is the name of, of, er, industry?
6. T: The music industry as, well, it's actually better

Sociocultural theories

Our final theory holds that learning a second language is very much a social activity, mediated by language. The original proponent of the theory was Vygotsky (1978), who said that learning takes place when there is an 'expert' knower who assists learners using language and dialogue. Learners pass through the **Zone of Proximal Development (ZPD)**, defined by Lantolf (2000: 17) as 'the collaborative construction of opportunities [...] for individuals to develop their mental abilities'. In other words, it is the extent to which individuals can develop their mental abilities by working together on a common task – here, learning new vocabulary. Central to that 'collaborative construction' is language.

When we apply this theory to the teaching of vocabulary, we see that learning occurs when individuals engage with a common task in the pursuit of a common goal. **Task-based** and **form-focused** instruction lie at the heart of this theoretical perspective. Learners must be given tasks to complete which are challenging, which require discussion and which help them to focus on *language*.

The lexical approach

One of the strongest arguments advanced for a teaching methodology which places vocabulary at its centre was advocated by Lewis (1993). His 'lexical approach' emphasises the importance of learning chunks of language which are made up of lexico-grammatical patterns. Many of these patterns are formulaic in nature and may therefore be transferred to other contexts. For example, if we teach 'do you mind if ...', learners can use this chunk to generate many other utterances in a wide range of contexts. The main advantage of the approach is that it can reduce communicative stress for the speaker or writer, making retrieval easier and improving fluency.

The lexical approach emphasises the teaching of set formulae which are then used to process new language and produce new utterances. Attention is given to *usefulness* rather than *frequency* and content words are given prominence.

In this chapter, we have seen how words are stored in the mind. In particular, we have seen that words are not stored in a random way, but are organised in some way in our minds. We also know that there is far more to 'knowing' a word than knowing its form and meaning; our knowledge of vocabulary is linked very closely with our knowledge of the world. When we recall a particular word like 'holidays', for example, we often have memories associated with that word. Recall of words is assisted by their *general shape* which gives us vital clues about their form, meaning and use. When we think of a word like 'immediately', for example, the predominant features are the beginning (*im-*) and end (*-ly*) of the word. This so-called *bathtub effect* (where the beginning and end of a word are prominent, but the middle 'dips') enables us to recall and use words more quickly. Fast recall of words and recalling words in chunks are vital to fluency and we therefore need to find ways of helping learners to store and retrieve words more efficiently.

Chapter review

1 In your own words, write a sentence to describe the mental lexicon. Why is it important?

2 What does it mean to 'know' a word? List five features, for example: 'knowing how to pronounce a word'.

3 Explain each of the following:
   a. input

   b. storage

   c. retrieval

4 Devise a semantic network for 'weather'.

5 List three strategies that teachers might use to help learners 'retrieve' vocabulary.

6 What are metacognitive strategies? Give an example.

7 Why is the negotiation of meaning important to vocabulary learning?

8 Give your own definition of each of the following and say why they are important for learning vocabulary:
   a. scaffolding

   b. ZPD

   c. form-focused instruction

9 How would you summarise the relationship between efficient storage and retrieval of words and spoken and written fluency?

10 What strategies can a teacher use to help learners recall words or find better alternatives?

10 | Words in society

TASK 1

Tick (✔) the box if you have seen these words before, and put another tick if you think you know what the word means:

	I have seen it	I think I know the meaning
rack rate		
subprime		
fanzine		
blogosphere		
blagger		

Vocabulary change

Vocabulary is constantly changing. Here are some words which were once used in English but are not used any more, and most people – apart from a few specialist scholars of the history of the language – have no idea of their meaning. We call these **archaisms**:

adjutorious   cerulific   diacle   ignic   tabard

Old words disappear, and only survive in old texts and in huge dictionaries such as the *Oxford English Dictionary* (*OED*). But new words are entering the language all the time, up to thousands every year. The *OED* publishes an update of new words online every three months, and these lists go into the hundreds! The words in Task 1 have all come from the *OED*'s lists in the last 50 years.

Change happens for a variety of reasons. The most obvious is related to changes in society and technology. A *tabard* (see the archaisms above) was a garment worn hundreds of years ago – no-one wears a tabard any more, and so the word has disappeared. Over the last 100 years, great changes have taken place in society. Cars, televisions, computers and other products of science and technology have all become commonplace in people's lives, and have brought with them thousands of new words. So, where do all these words come from, and how are they formed?

It may surprise you to know that very few words are absolutely new, created out of nothing. Most new words are either:

- new combinations of existing morphemes
- new combinations of existing words which make new compounds
- words made up by other processes which we looked at in Chapter 1, such as acronyms and blends
- words borrowed from other languages, or
- new meanings given to existing words.

We can see examples of all of these in the vocabulary of computers:

Word	Process of formation
incomputable	prefix -*in* + compute + suffix -*able*: existing morphemes
clipart	clip + art: compound
blog	(we)b + log: blend
wiki	from Hawaiian (meaning 'quickly'): borrowing
mouse	new meaning for an existing word

Sometimes the processes of formation are quite complex: the term *blogosphere* (meaning the area of the Internet where people post and read blogs) is a double blend, including part of the word *web*, the whole of the word *log* and the last part of the word *atmosphere*. Other examples of blends from areas of technology outside computers include *hi-viz jacket* (*hi-viz = high + visibility*) and *sat nav* systems (*satellite + navigation*) for vehicle navigation. These terms are invented by scientists and others involved in the technological world, as well as advertisers and marketers, to make it possible to communicate about the technological processes, to sell products and to make it easier for the population to use the technology. A computer 'mouse' is a good metaphor: a mouse with a cable looks a bit like a real mouse with a tail. Other computer metaphors include *surfing the Web*, *unzipping a file* and *downloading*; new, creative metaphors give rise to new language.

Apart from science and technology, other powerful forces at work in society include globalisation and the increased mobility of peoples, so that borrowing between languages has become more common. Because of the world dominance of English at this point in history, many languages include words borrowed from English, especially technical ones. But English itself borrows wholesale from other cultures, for example in the areas of food, as people travel and experiment with new cuisines. For most British and Irish people, words such as *tikka, biriani, vindaloo* and other names for varieties of Indian sub-continent curry dishes have become as ordinary and as English as any other words. Likewise, the influence of Hispanic culture in North America has made food words such as *nachos, enchiladas* and *salsa* commonplace in people's daily lives.

The influence of the media

TASK 2

Below are words and phrases (in **bold**) which we hear a lot on television. Do you know what they mean? Do you ever use them? With whom?

A: Want some dinner?
B: **Meh**, I'm not hungry.

A: Jason, you have to do your homework.
B: **Talk to the hand.**
Rotterdam is in Holland not Germany. **D'oh!**

A: We could go to the cinema on Friday night if you like.
B: **Whatever.**

Some of these words, *meh* (from 'mediocre', an expression of indifference, meaning 'I don't care') and *d'oh* (an exclamation used when someone has said or done something stupid), are made up words that first appeared on the long-running American animation show *The Simpsons*. As testimony to the power of the media as an agent of language change, these made-up words are now used internationally, especially among young people and they are also entries in the latest editions of a number of dictionaries. The phrase *talk to the hand* is also commonly used by young speakers. It originated in American urban sub-cultures but, through its use in various films and television shows, it spread to other varieties of English, especially within youth cultures. The phrase *whatever* is also from American youth culture, as well as popular TV shows, and it has also been adopted into other varieties of English.

VOCABULARY FILE

What is notable about *meh, d'oh!, talk to the hand* and *whatever* is that they have to be used with care. They can be, and are often meant to be, offensive.

In addition to initiating the use of new words, the popularity of international TV shows within certain age groups has also led to changes in patterns of existing words (see Chapter 4). The patterns do not necessarily originate in these TV programmes. The programmes merely mirror uses of language in society (or at least among certain groups). Here are three examples of usage commonly heard on such shows:

So
Old usage: adverb meaning 'very' used to modify adjectives
*It's **so** cold.*
*I'm **so** tired.*
*That music is **so** loud.*

New usage: intensifying adverb used to modify any word, phrase or clause.

*I'm **so** not buying you a birthday present.*

*That phone is **so** yesterday.*

*Your hair is **so** Tina Turner.*

How

Old usage: *How* + adjective + pronoun + verb *be*

***How** strange he is!*

***How** wonderful this is!*

***How** kind you are.*

New usage: *How* + adjective + verb *be* + pronoun

***How** strange is he!*

***How** ridiculous is that!*

***How** weird is that!*

Like

Old usage: a verb with a number of meanings including to enjoy, to want and (to look) similar to.

*I **like** coffee with cream.*

*I'd **like** to buy a new coat.*

*She looks **like** her mother.*

New usage: a reporting verb used with the verb *be* in the pattern: verb *be* + *like*

*I'm **like** 'No, I'm not going with you'*

*She **was like**, '£30 is too much!'*

*We're **like** 'whatever!'.*

Love

Old usage: to like very much, not used in the progressive form

*I **love** bagels with cream cheese.*

*We **love** living in the country.*

*Everybody is going to **love** this movie.*

New usage: to like very much, used in the progressive form

*Greg **is loving** his new job.*

*I'm not **loving** this soup.*

*We're **loving** the new project.*

Other media also have a rapid influence on how we use language, such as the Internet and SMS (Short Message Service) – or text messaging – via mobile phones. Through social networking sites, blogs and SMS, we write to people in pseudo-real time, and what we write is often closer to spoken rather than written language. A writer traditionally wrote for an audience that would read the text at a later time. Social networks, blogs and SMS messaging create a sense of simulated nearness between the writer and the reader. This makes the language more informal and often more intimate. The immediacy and informality of these new media have had two major influences on language: firstly, we try to make written language sound more like speaking and, secondly, we try to shorten words and sentences so as to speed up the transmission of our message (especially in real-time SMS or instant messaging).

For each of these text messages, write out the full normal written sentence and identify how each one has been made more like spoken language.

Text message	Full message	What makes it more like spoken language?
Will b n twn l8r. u on 4 it?		
Thx 4 CD. C u soon ☺		
Hope ur feelin ok.		
r u online?		

Language and social life

Here are four ways of describing a dog. Why are they different?

canine mammal　　　dog　　　doggy　　　bow-wow

Vocabulary both influences and reflects the way we live, as well as our history. We noted in Chapter 1, for example, that the vocabulary of English had been overlaid at various points in its history so that, nowadays, we have words which originated in the Anglo-Saxon world and in northern Europe generally, as well as words which had their origin in southern Europe, in the worlds of Ancient Greek and Latin and the medieval world. These two vocabularies do not simply exist side-by-side; they fulfil different social functions. The Anglo-Saxon and northern vocabulary accounts for many old, day-to-day words such as *man, tree, window, home*. In many cases, it is considered less formal than the Greek-Latin based vocabulary, which is the one most widely used in science and technology and in learning in general. So, often, we find a division between formal and informal language which reflects this history.

more formal	*more informal*
commence	start
increase	go up
quercus	oak tree
protrude	stick out

The difference between the two versions in each case is not one of correctness; it is one of appropriateness to different situations, in other words, a difference of register (see Chapter 2).

Register is a matter of who we are speaking or writing to, where and for what reason. It would be inappropriate and would sound rather pompous to say to one's dinner guests at the beginning of the meal 'Please commence!'; most people would simply say 'Please start!', which not only sounds more natural in that situation but it also creates the desired friendly atmosphere and reinforces a good relationship.

Speech and writing

One of the most important differences in register concerns whether we are speaking or writing. Words are often much more frequent in one type of communication than others. If we look at the frequencies of some words in written and spoken sections of the Bank of English corpus, we can see how differently they are distributed. The frequency figures are per ten million words.

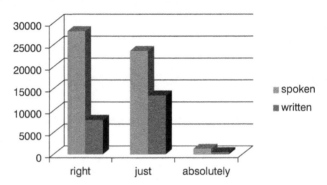

We can explain the differences in this chart by the fact that *right* is used as a discourse marker in spoken language (*Right! Let's get started!*) but not in written language; that *just* is used very often in spoken language to soften what we say to someone (*Can I just ask you a question?*) and that *absolutely* is often used in spoken language as an emphatic form of *yes* (*A: Did you think it was a good movie? B: Absolutely!*). In other cases, we can see the Greek-Latin versus Anglo-Saxon division reflected in speech and writing. In some other cases, certain derived forms of words are rarer than others. So, in the chart below, *commence* appears much less frequently in spoken language than in written language, and the adverb form *rightly* is far less common than *right* in all types of language, but especially so in spoken language:

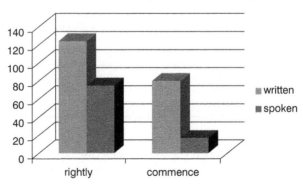

McCarthy and Carter (1997) give further information on the differences in frequency of common words in written and spoken English.

As well as their origins, there are other characteristics which give words a spoken or written flavour and associate them with different registers. For example, certain suffixes suggest more informal or conversational language. The *-y* suffix (as in *doggy* in Task 2) is often associated with friendly informality or with talking to children, and some noun forms even have spellings which give a clue to their change of register. Here are some examples:

word	word + -y suffix
biscuit	biccy
picture	piccy
cigarette	ciggy
frog	froggy

The *-y* suffix is often also associated with informal adjectives such as *comfy, freaky, stroppy, grumpy, yucky*, all of which have more formal equivalents (for example, *comfy/comfortable, stroppy/bad-tempered, yucky/disgusting*). The *-ish* suffix (used to make approximations) is similarly associated with informality (*she's thirty-ish, come about seven-ish*).

Mind your language!

Words are not just innocent 'containers' which have meaning; words also have associations and restrictions on their use. Some words are considered taboo (for example, slang words for parts of the human body, or slang words for sexual acts), and should never be used in polite society, while other words are considered sexist or 'politically incorrect'. Sexist language means language which suggests that one sex is more important than or superior to another, and sexist words often offend many people. For example, some traditional jobs and occupations were always done by one of the sexes, so words ending in *-man* and *-master/-mistress* were common, or else words ending in suffixes such as *-er/or* or *-ess*. Nowadays, both sexes do most occupations, and so more gender-neutral words are preferred:

old name	neutral name
fireman	fire-fighter
stewardess/air hostess	cabin attendant
headmaster/headmistress	headteacher
manager/manageress	manager (for both sexes)
waiter/waitress	server or waitron

Political correctness refers to the way words may become offensive to certain groups in society and so they are avoided; for example, words that refer to physical disabilities or to sexual orientation, race or religion. In order to avoid offending social groups, new ways of referring to people and things are adopted, and such ways can change over the years. Some examples from English in the last 50 years or so include:

now politically incorrect	politically correct
cripple	disabled person
queer	gay/homosexual
religions	faiths
backward child	child with learning difficulties
unmarried mother	lone parent/single parent
(red) Indian	Native American

Questions of sexism and political correctness demand great sensitivity of language users, and it must be remembered that the offence is in the ear and eye of the listener or reader (for more on sexism and political correctness in language, see Mills, 2008).

Words also have connotations, that is, they are associated with particular feelings or positive or negative emotions, so, for example, some of the idioms we looked at in Chapter 6 have negative associations (see also Chapter 2). If we say *pass the buck* (meaning pass the responsibility) we are always critical of someone. We would not say, *When old Mr Jones died, he passed the buck to his son,* if we mean he passed on the responsibility of running a successful family business (in a positive way). On the other hand, we would not say that someone was a *dab hand at something* (meaning they are very skilled at doing something, in a positive way) if we really meant they were skilled or expert fraudsters or thieves. Good dictionaries give information about connotations and associations of this kind, and it is part of the knowledge of native speakers and expert users to know what the connotations of a word or expression are. The tendency of words always to be used in particular kinds of context (negative situations or positive situations) is sometimes called semantic prosody (see Tognini-Bonelli, 2001: p.111ff.); the semantic prosody of words and expressions is part of the native speaker's and expert user's knowledge, even though it may only be unconscious knowledge.

PART B What are the problems for learners?

TASK 5

Why might learners have problems with these pairs of words?

pavement	sidewalk
children	offspring
bolshy	difficult

Native speakers and expert users of a language have had years of exposure to vocabulary (in the case of native speakers, probably since birth), so they develop a good instinct for knowing when a word is new or unusual or an archaism. Learners might not have the same instinct for the status of a word: they may not know if it is new, an archaism or if it is an established word they simply have not seen before. Therefore it is important for learners to be trained in using resources where they can find out about new or unusual words. The main resource will be the learners' dictionary. If a word is not in the learners' dictionary, then it is probably a rare word, an archaism or quite new. Learners can also do Web searches to see if the word is listed as a new word by the *OED* or some other reliable source. If learners are given awareness-training in the kinds of areas where new words are likely to occur (as in the examples we discussed earlier), they may be more sensitive to new words. Conversely, if they are reading classic works of literature, they will need to be more aware that words may be archaic and not used any more.

Perhaps a bigger problem for learners in their day-to-day encounters with English is knowing the variety and register of a word. Is the word American, Australian, British, Indian, Irish, Caribbean or another variety of English? Once again, a good learners' dictionary should give information about variety. The *Collins COBUILD Advanced Dictionary* (2009), for example, uses the abbreviation [AM] to label American-English words and gives the British English alternatives alongside them, so American-British equivalents like *elevator* and *lift*, *sidewalk* and *pavement* are clearly differentiated. As we mentioned in Chapter 3, learners often do not know about or do not use a lot of the excellent information in learners' dictionaries (Béjoint, 1981), and dictionary-training is essential.

The register of words is also an important area for learners, and one which can cause difficulties.

VOCABULARY FILE

Training learners to become aware of register is crucial, and involves developing sensitivity to areas such as Anglo-Saxon versus Greek-Latin vocabulary, differences between formal and informal usage, between speech and writing, and to features of word-formation which may give important information as regards a word's register (such as word-length or the inclusion of certain prefixes and suffixes).

It has been shown that learners in academic contexts often sound too 'chatty' in their written work, in other words, they import words and expressions from the spoken language into the written language (Gilquin and Paquot, 2008), and so, training in awareness of how 'spoken' or 'written' new words are used may be necessary. And, as we saw above, learners will also need to be sensitive to whether a word is taboo, or sexist, or politically incorrect if they do not want to offend people. With the globalising effect of television and the Internet, learners are increasingly being exposed to words (such as *meh, talk to the hand* and so on, as discussed in Section A) and patterns of use (such as *I'm like..., This is so yesterday*) which do not appear in their textbooks and which can at times be considered offensive or incorrect, especially in test situations. This poses the challenge of knowing when, how and whether to use these words and patterns.

Knowing the variety and register of a word is part of the learner's **depth of knowledge,** which we can contrast with **breadth of knowledge** (Wesche and Paribakht,

1996). Breadth of knowledge means, roughly speaking, how many words you know with their basic meanings. Depth of knowledge means: what do you know about those words? In other words, depth of knowledge means having different kinds of information about words, such as their grammar (see Chapter 7), their collocations (see Chapter 3) and their register (see Chapter 2). Once the first 2000 words have been mastered (see Chapter 1), it becomes more and more important to move from just increasing the learner's breadth of vocabulary to increasing their depth of knowledge.

The problem of dealing with varieties and registers for learners will include the question of whether **receptive knowledge** is sufficient or whether **productive knowledge** is also important. Receptive knowledge of a word, according to Nation (1990: 31–32) includes knowing whether it is common or rare or archaic, and knowing its variety and register. Armed with receptive knowledge, the learner can then apply this as productive knowledge – is it appropriate to use the word in this particular text, in this particular register, to this particular person and so on?

PART C How do we teach it?

TASK 6

Think of two ways you could tackle the problem of teaching the register of words in class.

Most of what we have discussed in this chapter concerns depth of vocabulary knowledge, that is to say, how much learners need to know *about* words, not just how many words they need to know, and we have focused on the social contexts of words as an important part of this knowledge. Much of this kind of deep knowledge will be more important for intermediate and advanced learners, but, as with all aspects of vocabulary learning, encouraging good learning habits from the very beginning is a good idea.

In class, teachers can use a variety of methods to raise awareness of the issues of words in society. For example, the teacher can find new words and compounds in English by doing a Web search at sites such as the *Oxford English Dictionary*'s homepage, and then showing these to more advanced students to test if they can see how the new words and compounds have been formed, even if they do not know their meaning. Students can discuss the new words in pairs or groups. As we discussed in Chapter 1, training in English word-formation processes can be a very good way of improving language awareness and of generating vocabulary-building resources. Students can also be encouraged to collect new words and expressions as they encounter them and then to check them in dictionaries or on the Internet to see if they can find out whether they are indeed new, or archaic, or established and currently used.

Working on registers in class can also be done in a variety of ways. Students can work in pairs or groups with pairs of words from contrasting registers, using dictionaries and any other resource such as the Internet to find out which registers they belong to. Clues or prompts can also be given if the exercise is difficult, for example:

Put each word in the correct box, depending on how it is normally used.

wireless   radio
controversy   rumpus
gas   petrol
old woman   old biddy
icky   unpleasant

pair 1	newspaper headlines	academic texts
pair 2	writing	conversation
pair 3	old-fashioned	present-day
pair 4	sexist	neutral
pair 5	British English	American English

Another way of dealing with register is to look at whole texts, or to compare pairs of texts. For example, a text from a popular newspaper could be compared with coverage of the same event from a quality newspaper, or a written short story could be compared with a spoken, informal anecdote. Also, using extracts from popular television programmes or films, social networking sites and blogs can also be a way of focusing on how people use language in informal contexts.

VOCABULARY FILE

Learners need to know that they will hear and read forms that are not in their textbooks. It is their choice whether they wish to use them but they need to know also that some of these words and phrases can be offensive and are only appropriate in informal communication between friends.

Increasing depth of vocabulary knowledge basically involves encouraging good learning strategies, and strategy training is crucial in the area of words in society. Schmitt (1997) has shown that learners use a wide range of strategies for dealing with new words, from looking for translations to using flash cards, to using dictionaries, to interacting with the teacher and asking questions. Generally speaking, the more a learner moves away from the basic core vocabulary which is necessary for survival, the more their simpler strategies should ideally be replaced by cognitively engaging ones, such as interacting in pairs and groups or discussing words with the teacher, or carrying out searches in various resources. In this way, depth of knowledge is likely to follow, whereas working alone with a simple, bilingual dictionary and direct translations is unlikely to lead to the same results, Such depth of knowledge will, hopefully, bring with it a growing sensitivity to register and other social aspects and connotations of words, including their semantic prosody.

Finally, when students are of a sufficient level of proficiency, they can engage with real data from corpora in the form of concordances (these can be accessed online at websites including the Bank of English or the British National Corpus), which the students can then discuss in class. This direct encounter with real language, data-driven learning, or DDL as it is called (see Chapters 2 and 9), turns the learner into a true researcher (Hadley, 2002). Here is an example of a concordance from the Limerick Corpus of Irish English. Each line shows a different occasion when speakers used the word *lucky*. The task for intermediate or advanced learners might be to study the concordance to see if *lucky* is a synonym for *happy*, which it is in some languages, but not in English. In some lines, *happy* could be used (line 1 or 7), but not in others (line 6 or 9). Additionally, learners could discuss the sorts of contexts *lucky* is used in (sports, superstitions about numbers, winning things, being given valuable things and so on).

1	the races tonight. Our James is really	**lucky**	but sure he's no winner yet.
2	around there for the day. But it was	**lucky**	when we got the ticket but and
3	On his head like and. I was very	**lucky**	that time I had the head injury yeah
4	the job that Tim didn't get. Yeah he's flipping	**lucky**	he didn't get it. Oh would he not have
5	best way to do it I'd say. You could be	**lucky**	like get a you know a nice. Yeah lovely
6	Liverpool as you said they got a very very	**lucky**	goal didn't they. They have great matches.
7	yeah madness. My brother now was very	**lucky**	His father-in-law gave him a plot of land
8	Was it really? Oh fabulous. You can be	**lucky**	and unlucky sometimes in those places.
9	left in for seven days because seven was a	**lucky**	number. Right. So you went over to her every day
10	He was in a very bad way. So we were	**lucky**	to get him over, you know. Right. A few hours

DDL, encouraging learners to interact about vocabulary and to negotiate meaning (see Chapter 9), along with a broad focus on learning words in their social contexts, encourages vocabulary learning strategies which will stand learners in good stead long after their course has ended, when there are still thousands of words and expressions to be learnt. Our goal as teachers should be to foster the independent vocabulary learner, the learner who knows what the vocabulary learning challenge is, makes it a lifelong quest and enjoys it. It is that learner we have had in mind throughout this book.

Chapter review

1 Explain in a sentence how words appear and disappear from the English language.

2 How are new words formed? Name three of the five processes described in Chapter 10.

3 How would you send the following as text messages? In what ways are the text messages different?

Message	Text message
See you later.	
I'll be arriving at about 10 AM.	
I'm busy right now, I'll call you later.	
I love you too.	

4 What is 'wrong' with each of these responses? Correct it and say why it was incorrect.

(1)
A. How are you?
B. *Well, actually, not so good. My head is killing me, my back's sore, I've been sneezing all day and I've had a bad cough all week. I think I'll have to make an appointment to see the doctor today, but then ...*

(2)
A. Would you like to come for a drink later?
B. *No.*

(3)
A. Are you busy?
B. *Yes.*

(4)
A. Have you got the time?
B. *Yes thanks.*

5 The following words are all used to describe someone's appearance. Which have positive connotations and which have negative ones? How did you decide?

skinny
well-made
lanky
matronly
long-limbed

6 Each of the following is rather archaic. Replace each one with a more contemporary version. What would you do if learners used 'old-fashioned' vocabulary?

It's raining cats and dogs.
How do you do?
He's an awfully nice chap.
We had a glorious time!
What a spiffing outfit!

7 What is this activity designed to teach and how would you use it in class?

Match a word in column A with a more neutral word in column B.

A	B
Hideous	Shining
Agony	Nice
Shuddering	Shaking
Glistening	Pain
Exquisite	Ugly
Quiver	Picked up
Seized	Tremble

8 Look again at the concordance line for lucky presented earlier in the chapter. How might you use this with a group of intermediate level learners?

9 Suggest three ways in which intermediate to advanced learners can learn *about* words.

10 Match the following words and phrases to the four registers listed below and suggest an alternative for each one in everyday English:

blaze   *conversely*   *youths*   *grow the profit margins*
make an incision   *empirical*   *recuperate*

(A) newspaper headline   (B) medical   (C) business   (D) academic

References

Aitchison, J. (1976) *The Articulate Mammal: An Introduction to Psycholinguistics*. London/ New York: Routledge.

Arnaud, P. and Savignon, S. (1977) 'Rare words, complex lexical units and the advanced learner'. In J. Coady and T. Huckin (eds), *Second Language Vocabulary Acquisition*, 157–200. Cambridge: Cambridge University Press.

Bates, D.R. and McCarroll, R. (1958) Proc. R. Soc. A245, 175 (unpublished dissertation). London: Hall.

Béjoint, H. (1981) 'The foreign student's use of monolingual English dictionaries'. *Applied Linguistics* 2(3): 207–22.

Bergstrom, K. (1979) 'Idioms exercises and speech activities to develop fluency'. *Collected Reviews*. Summer: 21–2.

Biber, D., Conrad, S. and Reppen, R. (1998) *Corpus Linguistics. Investigating Language Structure and Use*. Cambridge: Cambridge University Press.

Biber, D., Johansson, S., Leech, G., Conrad, S. and Finegan, E. (1999) *Longman Grammar of Spoken and Written English*. London: Longman.

Boers, F. (2007) 'Presenting figurative idioms with a touch of etymology: more than mere mnemonics?' *Language Teaching Research*, 11(1): 43–62.

Bolinger, D. (1976) 'Meaning and memory'. *Forum Linguisticum*, 1: 2–14.

Breen, M.P. (1998) 'Navigating the discourse: on what is learned in the language classroom'. In W.A. Renandya and G.M. Jacobs (eds) *Learners and Language Learning*. Anthology Series 39. Singapore: SEAMO Regional Language Centre.

Bygate, M. (1988) *Speaking*. Oxford: Oxford University Press.

Cambridge International Dictionary of Idioms (1998). Cambridge: Cambridge University Press.

Cameron, L. (2001) *Teaching Languages to Young Learners*. Cambridge: Cambridge University Press.

Carter, R.A. (1987) *Vocabulary in Language Teaching*. London: Longman.

Carter, R. and McCarthy, M.J. (2006) *The Cambridge Grammar of English*. Cambridge: Cambridge University Press.

Cervatiuc, A. (2008) 'ESL Vocabulary Acquisition: Target and Approach'. *The Internet TESL Journal* XIV(1), January 2008.

Charteris-Black, J. (2002) 'Second Language Figurative Proficiency: A Comparative Study of Malay & English'. *Applied Linguistics*, 23(1): 104–33.

Chomsky, N. (1965) *Aspects of the Theory of Syntax*. Boston: MIT Press.

Cobb, T. (1997) Is there any measurable learning from hands-on concordancing? *System*, 25(3): 301–15.

COBUILD (2007) *Collins COBUILD Advanced Dictionary of American English*. Boston: Thomson Heinle.

COBUILD (2009) *Collins COBUILD Advanced Dictionary*. Glasgow: HarperCollins.

Cook, G. (1989) *Discourse*. Oxford: Oxford University Press.

Cooper, T.C. (1999) 'Processing of Idioms in L2 Learners of English'. *TESOL Quarterly*, 33(2): 233–62.

Crystal, D. (2003) *Cambridge Encyclopedia of the English Language*. Cambridge: Cambridge University Press.
Cunningsworth, A. (1995) *Choosing Your Coursebook*. London: Macmillan.

de Saussure, F. (1974) *Course in General Linguistics*. London: Fontana.

Ellis, N. (1995) 'Vocabulary acquisition: the implicit ins and outs of explicit cognitive mediation'. In N. Ellis (ed.), *Implicit and Explicit Learning of Languages*. London and San Diego: Academic Press.
Ellis, N. (ed.) (1995) *Implicit and Explicit Learning of Languages*. London: Academic Press.
Ellis, R. (1994) *The Study of Second Language Acquisition*. Oxford: Oxford University Press.
Ellis, R. (1997) *Second Language Acquisition*. Oxford: Oxford University Press.

Farghal, M. and Obiedar, H. (1995) Collocations: A neglected variable in EFL. *International Review of Applied Linguistics in Language Teaching (IRAL)*, 33: 315–31.
Farr, F., Murphy, B. and O'Keeffe, A. (2002) 'The Limerick Corpus of Irish English: Design, description and application'. *Teanga* 21: 5–29.

Gilquin, G. and Paquot, M. (2008) 'Too chatty: Learner academic writing and register variation'. *English Text Construction*, 1(1): 41–61.
Giora, R. (2003) *On Our Mind: Salience, Context, and Figurative Language*. New York: Oxford University Press.
Granger, S. (1998) 'Prefabricated patterns in advanced EFL writing: Collocations and formulae'. In A.P. Cowie (ed.) *Phraseology: Theory, analysis, and application*. Oxford: Clarendon Press, 145–60.
Grice, P. (1975) 'Logic and conversation'. In *Syntax and Semantics, 3: Speech Acts*, P. Cole and J. Morgan (eds). New York: Academic Press.

Hadley, G. (2002) 'Sensing the winds of change: An introduction to data-driven learning'. *RELC Journal* 33(2): 99–124.
Halliday, M.A.K. (1978) *Language as Social Semiotic*. London: Edward Arnold.
Halliday, M.A.K. and Hasan, R. (1976) *Cohesion in English*. London: Longman.
Hoey, M. (1991) *Patterns of Lexis in Text*. Oxford: Oxford University Press.
Howarth, P. (1998) 'The phraseology of learners' academic writing'. In A.P. Cowie (ed.), *Phraseology, Theory, Analysis, and Application*, 161–86. Oxford: Clarendon Press.
Hunston, S. and Francis, G. (2000) *Pattern Grammar: A Corpus-driven Approach to the Lexical Grammar of English*. Amsterdam: John Benjamins.

Irujo, S. (1986) 'A piece of cake: learning and teaching idioms'. *ELT Journal*, 40(3): 236–42.

Kellerman, E. (1986) 'An eye for an eye: Crosslinguistic constraints on the development of the L2 lexicon'. In E. Kellerman and M. Sharwood Smith (eds), *Crosslinguistic Influence in Second Language Acquisition*, 35–48. Oxford: Pergamon Press.
Krashen, S. (1989) 'We acquire vocabulary and spelling by reading: Additional evidence for the input hypothesis'. *Modern Language Journal*, 73: 440–64.
Krashen, S. and Terrell, T. (1983) *The Natural Approach: Language Acquisition in the Classroom*. New York: Prentice Hall.

Lakoff, G. and Johnson, M. (1980) *Metaphors We Live By*. Chicago: University of Chicago.
Lantolf, J.P. (2000) *Sociocultural Theory and Second Language Learning*. Oxford: Oxford University Press.
Lattey, E. (1986) 'Pragmatic classification of idioms as an aid for the language learner'. *International Review of Applied Linguistics*, XXIV(3): 217–33.

Leech, G., Rayson, P. and Wilson, A. (2001) *Word Frequencies in Written and Spoken English*. Harlow: Pearson Education.

Lewis, M. (1993) *The Lexical Approach: The State of ELT and the Way Forward*. Hove: Language Teaching Publications

Lewis, M. (2002) *The Lexical Approach*. Boston: Thomson Heinle.

Long, M.H. (1983) 'Native Speaker/Non-native Speaker Conversation and the Negotiation of Meaning'. *Applied Linguistics*, 4: 126–41.

Long, M.H. (1996) 'The Role of the Linguistic Environment in Second Language Acquisition'. In W.C. Ritchie and T.K. Bhatia (eds) *Handbook of Second Language Acquisition*. San Diego: Academic Press.

Longman (1998) *Longman Idioms Dictionary*. Harlow: Longman ELT.

Longman (2007) *Longman Business English Dictionary*. Harlow: Longman ELT.

LTP (1997) *LTP Dictionary of Selected Collocations*. Hove: Language Teaching Publications.

Macmillan (2002) *Macmillan English Dictionary for Advanced Learners*. Oxford: Macmillan Education.

Marks, J. and Wooder, A. (2007) *Check Your Vocabulary for Natural English Collocations*. London: A & C Black.

McCarthy, M.J. (1990) *Vocabulary*. Oxford: Oxford University Press.

McCarthy, M.J. (1991) *Discourse Analysis for Language Teachers*. Cambridge: Cambridge University Press.

McCarthy, M.J. (1995 reprint) *Vocabulary*. Oxford: Oxford University Press.

McCarthy, M.J. (1998) *Spoken Language and Applied Linguistics*. Cambridge: Cambridge University Press.

McCarthy, M.J. and Carter, R.A. (1997) 'Written and spoken vocabulary'. In N. Schmitt and M.J. McCarthy (eds), *Vocabulary: Description, Acquisition, Pedagogy*, 20–39. Cambridge: Cambridge University Press.

McCarthy, M.J., McCarten, J. and Sandiford, H. (2005) *Touchstone. Student's Book 1*. Cambridge: Cambridge University Press.

McCarthy, M.J., McCarten, J. and Sandiford, H. (2006) *Touchstone. Student's Book 4*. Cambridge: Cambridge University Press.

McCarthy, M.J and O'Dell, F. (1999) *English Vocabulary in Use. Elementary*. Cambridge: Cambridge University Press.

McCarthy, M.J and O'Dell, F. (2001) *English Vocabulary in Use. Upper-intermediate*. Cambridge: Cambridge University Press.

McCarthy, M.J. and O'Dell, F. (2002) *English Idioms in Use*. Cambridge: Cambridge University Press.

McCarthy, M.J. and O'Dell, F. (2005) *English Collocations in Use*. Cambridge: Cambridge University Press.

McCarthy, M., O'Keeffe, A. and Walsh, S. (2007) *ELT Advantage*. Boston: Thomson Heinle.

McLay, V. (1987) *Idioms at Work*. Hove: Language Teaching Publications.

Mezynski, K. (1983) 'Issues concerning the acquisition of knowledge: Effects of vocabulary training on reading comprehension'. *Review of Educational Research*, 53: 253–79.

Mills, S. (2008) *Language and Sexism*. Cambridge: Cambridge University Press.

Moon, R. (1987) 'The analysis of meaning'. In J. Sinclair, *Looking up: An account of the COBUILD project in Lexical Computing*, 86–103. [2.1]. London: Collins.

Nation, I.S.P. (1990) *Teaching and Learning Vocabulary*. Boston: Heinle and Heinle.

Nation, P. and Waring, R. (1997) 'Vocabulary Size, Text Coverage and Word Lists'. In N. Schmitt and McCarthy M. (eds), *Vocabulary: Description, Acquisition and Pedagogy*, 6–19. Cambridge: Cambridge University Press.

Nelson, C. and Harper, V. (2006) 'A Pedagogy of Difficulty: Preparing Teachers To Understand and Integrate Complexity in Teaching and Learning'. *Teacher Education Quarterly*. Spring, 1–3.

Nunan, D. (2003) *Practical English Language Teaching*. New York: McGraw Hill.

O'Dell, F. and McCarthy, M.J. (2008) *English Collocations in Use. Advanced*. Cambridge: Cambridge University Press.

O'Keeffe, A., McCarthy, M.J. and Carter, R. (2006) *From Corpus to Classroom*. Cambridge: Cambridge University Press.

OUP (2006) *Oxford Collocations Dictionary for Students of English*. Oxford: Oxford University Press.

OUP (2006) *Oxford Idioms Dictionary for Learners of English*. Oxford: Oxford University Press.

Oxford, R. (1990) *Language learning strategies: What every teacher should know*. Boston: Heinle and Heinle.

Palmer, H. (1925) *The Oral Method of Teaching Languages*. Cambridge.

Pawley, A. and Syder, F. (1983) 'Two puzzles for linguistic theory: Nativelike selection and nativelike fluency'. In J.C. Richards and R.W. Schmidt (eds), *Language and Communication*, 191–226. London: Longman.

Peters, A.M. (1983) *The Units of Language Acquisition*. Cambridge: Cambridge University Press.

Plag, I. (2003) *Word Formation in English*. Cambridge: Cambridge University Press.

Römer, U. (2005) *Progressives, Patterns, Pedagogy: A Corpus-driven Approach to English Progressive Forms, Functions, Contexts and Didactics*. Amsterdam: John Benjamins.

Ryan, A. and Meara, P. (1991) 'The case of the invisible vowels: Arabic speakers reading English words'. *Reading in a Foreign Language* 7: 531–40.

Sacks, H. (1972) 'An Initial Investigation of the Usability of Conversational Data for Doing Sociology'. In D. Sudnow (ed.), *Studies in Social Interaction*, 31–74. New York: The Free Press.

Schmitt, N. (1997) Vocabulary learning strategies. In Schmitt, N. and McCarthy, M.J. (eds), *Vocabulary: Description, Acquisition, Pedagogy*, 199–227. Cambridge: Cambridge University Press.

Schmitt, N. and Zimmerman, C.B. (2002) 'Derivative Word Forms: What Do Learners Know?' *TESOL Quarterly* 36(2): 145–71.

Schmitt, N. and Schmitt, D. (1995) 'Vocabulary notebooks: theoretical underpinnings and practical suggestions'. *ELT Journal* 49(2): 133–43

Simpson, R. and Mendis, D. (2003) 'A corpus-based study of idioms in academic speech'. *TESOL Quarterly* 37(3): 419–41.

Sinclair, J. (1987) *Looking up: An account of the COBUILD project in Lexical Computing*. London: Collins.

Sinclair, J. (1991) *Corpus, Concordance, Collocation*. Oxford: Oxford University Press.

Skinner, B.F. (1953) *Science and Human Behaviour*. New York: The Free Press.

Spöttl, C. and McCarthy, M.J. (2004) 'Comparing the knowledge of formulaic sequences across L1, L2, L3 and L4'. In Schmitt, N. (ed.), *Formulaic Sequences*, 191–225. Amsterdam: John Benjamins.

Stahl, S.A. and Fairbanks, M.M. (1986) 'The effects of vocabulary instruction: A model-based meta-analysis'. *Review of Educational Research*, 56: 72–110.

Taiwo, R. (2004) 'Helping ESL learners to minimise collocational errors'. *The Internet TESL Journal*, X(4).

Thomson, W.R. (1995) 'Coincidence Studies of Collisions of Electrons and Ions with Oxygen'. Unpublished thesis, Queen's University, Belfast.

Tognini-Bonelli, E. (2001) *Corpus Linguistics at Work*. Amsterdam: John Benjamins.

Ur, P. (1996). *A Course in Language Teaching*. Cambridge: Cambridge University Press.

Vygotsky, L.S. (1978) *Mind in Society: The Development of Higher Psychological Processes*. Boston: Harvard University Press.

Wajnryb, R. (1990) *Resource Books for Teachers: Grammar Dictation*. Oxford: Oxford University Press.

Walsh, S. (2001) 'Characterising teacher talk in the second language classroom: a process model of reflective practice'. Unpublished PhD, Queen's University, Belfast.

Walsh, S. (2002) 'Construction or obstruction: teacher talk and learner involvement in the EFL classroom'. *Language Teaching Research*, 6(1): 3–23.

Walsh, S. (2007) Learner Corpus of Dissertation Writing. Author's own unpublished corpus.

Walsh, S. and O'Keeffe, A. (2007) 'Applying CA to a modes analysis of third-level spoken academic discourse'. In Bowles, P. and Seedhouse, P. (eds), *Conversation Analysis and Languages for Specific Purposes*, 101–39. Berlin: Peter Lang.

Ward, J. (2007) 'Collocation and technicality in EAP engineering'. *Journal of English for Academic Purposes*, 6(1): 18–35.

Watts, R.J. (2003) *Politeness*. Cambridge: Cambridge University Press.

Wesche, M. and Paribakht, T.S. (1996) 'Assessing second language vocabulary knowledge: Depth versus breadth'. *The Canadian Modern Language Review*, 53(1): 13–40.

Widdowson, H.G. (1983) *Learning Purpose and Language Use*. Oxford: Oxford University Press.

Willis, D. (2006) *Teaching Lexical Phrases and Lexical Patterns*. Paper read at TESOL Paris, November 2006. Available online.

Wray, A. (2000) 'The functions of formulaic language: an integrated model'. *Language and Communication*, 20(1): 1–28.

Wray, A. (2002) *Formulaic Language and the Lexicon*. Cambridge: Cambridge University Press.

Wright, J. (1999) *Idioms Organiser*. Hove: Language Teaching Publications.

Yorio, C.A. (1989) 'Idiomaticity as an indicator of second language proficiency'. In Hyltenstam, K. and Obler, L. (eds), *Bilingualism Across the Lifespan*, 55–69. Cambridge: Cambridge University Press.

Task commentaries

Chapter 1

TASK 1

How many words are there on each line? Write in your answers, as in the examples.

car	1
car park	2
it's	1
pre-school	1
prejudge	1
forgetful	1

This task makes you think about exactly what a word is. Car is obviously one word, and car park is two, because there is a space between car and park. But what about *it's*? We know it means *it is*, so is it two words? It is written as one word (condensed and indicated by the apostrophe '), so it is just one word. Pre-school has a hyphen, so we also consider that to be one word, even though it has two parts. Prejudge and forgetful also have different parts within them, but they are still written as one word. The task shows how there is not one simple answer to the question 'What is a word?'

TASK 2

waste paper basket	3
desktop	1
blog	1
phone	1
DVD	1
look looks looking looked	See the commentary

Task 2 is similar to Task 1. Waste paper basket is written as three words, even though it means just one thing in the real world. Desktop is also written as one word, even though we can see two words in it. Blog is one word, but in fact it's made up of bits of other words (web and log). Phone is one word, but it's only part of the longer word telephone. DVD stands for three words (digital versatile disc) but we write it as one. The different forms of the verb 'look' are written as different words, but we know they are all part of the same lexical item, *look*. We can say that these are word-forms which are all part of the same word-family. Once again, the way we write words is actually quite complex, and there is no simple answer to the question 'What is a word?'.

1 In the biggest dictionaries, for example the famous Oxford English Dictionary (OED), there can be half a million or more English words – though it depends, of course, on what counts as a 'word'.

2 We don't know exactly, and estimates vary, but it is certainly tens of thousands of words, perhaps around 50 000.

3 To survive in everyday conversation, there is a core of about 2000 words which are used and re-used, and they are sufficient for most ordinary conversation, although we also need special words if we want to talk about our special individual interests.

TASK 4

There are many things which could be problematic for learners. Here are just four:

1 Knowing how to spell and pronounce words, since English spelling and pronunciation are not regular.

2 Knowing whether to write a compound as one word or more than one, or when to use a hyphen, as there are very few fixed rules for such usage.

3 Knowing which words are important to learn and which words are rare.

4 Knowing whether you can use a particular prefix in front of a word; for example, we can say unpopular but can we say unpolite? In fact we can't – the opposite of polite is impolite.

Chapter 2

Tasks 1, 2, 8 are dealt with in the body of the text.

TASK 3   *bank, tap, bat*

TASK 4   A good dictionary should be able to provide at least 15 meanings of *take*.

TASK 5   *menu*: old meaning = food options in a restaurant; new meaning = set of choices within a computer program

notepad: old meaning = a block of paper usually used for letter writing; new meaning = laptop

click = a short sharp sound made with one's fingers or mouth; new meaning = to press a button on a computer mouse

spam: old meaning = a type of canned meat usually made from pork; new meaning = unwanted emails or 'junk' emails

site: old meaning = a particular place where something is (to be) built or where something important happened in the past, such as a battle site; new meaning = a web page or website at a particular URL (web address)

web: old meaning = what a spider builds; new meaning = another word for the Internet

TASK 6

eagle
denotative meaning: *a large bird with a curved beak which hunts small animals*
connotative meaning: (possible answer) *an eagle has the connotation of power and strength*
Was the connotative meaning which you described personal or held by a group of people, culture or society?
(possible answer) *This connotation of an eagle as a symbol of power and strength is cultural, mostly related to its use in the USA.*

heart
denotative meaning: *the organ in your chest which sends blood around your body*
connotative meaning: (possible answer) *a heart has the connotation of love*
Was the connotative meaning which you described personal or held by a group of people, culture or society?
(possible answer) *Cultural but very universal*

feminist
denotative meaning: *a person, usually a woman, who believes in and supports equal rights and opportunities for women in society.*
connotative meaning: (possible answer) *an angry strident woman*
Was the connotative meaning you have described personal or held by a group of people, culture or society?
(possible answer) *personal*

Paris
denotative meaning: *The capital city of France*
connotative meaning: (possible answer) *a place of romance*
Was the connotative meaning which you described personal or held by a group of people, culture or society?
(possible answer) *Societal*

hitchhiking
denotative meaning: *to get around by putting your thumb out while on the side of the road and getting lifts from cars and other vehicles without paying*
connotative meaning: (possible answer) *student*
Was the connotative meaning which you described personal or held by a group of people, culture or society?
(possible answer) *Societal – in my country, students hitchhike.*

TASK 7

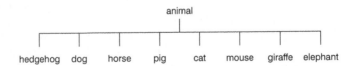

TASK 8

1 Register: medical.

Words which suggest register: *radiological; stage-2, stage-3 lesions; mean interval; onset; tumour; detection; lung; metastases.*

2 Register: academic (a computer science lecture).

Words which suggest register: (possible answer) *Okay, today I want to talk to you about operating systems.*

3 Register: cookery (a recipe).

Words which suggest register: *chop, lamb, cubes, marinade, aromatic, spices, sweat, onion, garlic, add, coconut, milk.*

4 Register: casual conversation.

Words which suggest register: (possible answer) the frequent use of *we* and the reference to people's first names and other casual expressions, for example, *here, we'll, Mark, Brian, having a laugh, boys, girls.*

TASK 9

Some of the new uses of hand that you may have found from the concordance lines might include:

1 *hand-held*: a device that can be used in your hand

2 *second-hand*: something that is not new and has been owned by someone else

3 *go hand-in-hand*: referring to things that usually go together

4 *hand*: prefix meaning by hand, for example, *hand-sliced* – sliced by hand rather than machine

5 *hand-harvested*: harvested by hand rather than machine, *hand-rolled*: rolled by hand rather than by machine, and so on

Chapter 3

TASK 1

heavy rain	N
heavy bag	N
heavy sunshine	U
strong wind	N
strong car	U
powerful car	N
blond hair	N
blond jacket	U

Although we often say heavy rain and heavy bag, heavy sunshine sounds very odd. Heavy and sunshine simply do not go together. Similarly, we talk about a powerful car rather than a strong car, and blond, as a colour, can only be used for people's hair, not for clothes or other objects. This task shows us that words have preferred ways of combining and that, if we know a language, we know what the preferred combinations are and which combinations are strange or unacceptable.

TASK 2

key word

| **very** | _noisy_ | _nice_ | _good_ | dead | _easy_ | _happy_ | _cold_ |
| **utterly** | _wrong_ | _stupid_ | hard | _ridiculous_ | hungry | old | _crazy_ |

This task shows us that very collocates with a lot of different words, but not adjectives which are either/or, such as dead or married (you are either dead or not dead, married or not married). *Utterly* collocates with subjective negative-critical words, but not usually objective descriptions such as hard or hungry or cold.

TASK 3

go *home (travel to one's home)*
get *a new computer (buy/obtain
    a new computer)*
make *dinner (cook/prepare dinner)*
catch *a bus (take a bus/get on a bus)*

go *crazy (become crazy)*
get *the phone (answer the phone)*
make *a noise (cause/create a noise)*
catch *a cold (contract a cold / become
infected with a cold)*

This task shows that some common, everyday verbs (such as *get, take*) have different meanings, depending on the nouns they collocate with. It is very difficult to say what the independent meanings of such verbs are; collocation is central to understanding them.

TASK 4

create a macro – computer English
close a deal – business English
submit a paper – academic English
custodial sentence – legal English
refute a hypothesis – academic English
balance the books – business English
award damages – legal English
overwrite a file – computer English

TASK 5

Some English courses include nothing at all about collocation, and many learners think vocabulary is only about learning individual words. However, some courses teach collocations but call them word pairs, or word partners, or word combinations. Some courses and books actually use the term collocation directly.

Chapter 4

Tasks 1, 2, 3 are dealt with in the body of the text.

TASK 4

Different patterns of *catch* in each register:

From the Limerick Corpus of Irish English:
Main pattern: *catch* + direct object (literal meaning 'to take hold of something')
Other less frequent patterns: *catch* + onto (phrasal verb meaning to become popular); didn't (quite) *catch* + that (meaning to hear or understand something, usually used in negative statements, that is when you do not hear of understand something)

From the Limerick-Belfast Corpus of Academic Spoken English
Main patterns: *Did/could* + *you* + *catch* + *it/that?* (metaphorical meaning 'to hear something' in the context of a class listening to an audio recording)
Catch + *up* (phrasal verb meaning to reach a certain standard)
The + *catch* (noun meaning a hidden problem)
Less frequent pattern: *catch* + *up* + *phase* used to modify noun *phase,* meaning a period where certain standards are reached.

Chapter 5

TASK 1

Affix and function	Examples
-ly (makes an adjective)	*quickly*
non- (makes a negative)	*non-starter*
in- (makes an opposite)	*inconvenient*
re- (means 'again')	*recast*
-ing (creates a 'gerund', a kind of noun)	*reading*
de- (means 'take away')	*devalue*
-s (makes plural)	*boys*

TASK 2

Give three examples of compounds for each combination below (15 words in total):

noun + noun	policeman, homework, saucepan, etc.
adjective + noun	sourdough, longboat, tallboy, etc.
verb + noun	call centre, playhouse, think-tank, etc.
verb + verb	play act, make believe, make do, etc.
verb + particle	dropout, sing along, freeze over, etc.

TASK 3

When we first encounter words like these, there may be a tendency to deconstruct them and this is a useful strategy to teach learners.

However, once words have become established, there is no need to deconstruct each time we meet the word. This would, in fact, prevent fluent communication and create problems.

TASK 4 Separable: *look over, put on, put through, put off, put up to.*
Inseparable: *look around, look up, look at, get up to, get on, get around to, get off, make do, make off with, make sure, make over.*

TASK 5 Some of these lexical chunks are used very frequently, while others are not. The guideline here is frequency and 'generalisability', or how widely used is the expression and how easy is it to transfer it from one context to another? The following all meet these two criteria and could therefore be selected for teaching purposes: *Nice to see you, what about you? See you, long time no see.* The remaining ones are used less frequently and have fewer applications to different contexts.

TASK 6 Typically, there are no literal translations for fixed or semi-fixed words like these. There is no one-for-one translation and no correspondence between literal and pragmatic meaning. Literal meaning is the actual meaning of words themselves, while pragmatic meaning refers to what happens to meaning when the words are used in a particular context. When learners encounter such vocabulary, they have to be given lots of examples to clarify both meaning and usage.

TASK 7 Although learner 7 (L7) seems to understand 'penalty shoot-out', there is no checking of meaning by involving other members of the class. Here, the teacher could have checked the meaning and asked for other examples using 'penalty shoot-out'. One contribution from one learner does not tell the teacher that the class understand. One way of checking learning is to use concept checking questions such as: *When do we see a penalty shoot out? What happens in a penalty shoot-out? How do we decide the winning team after a penalty shoot-out?* In this way, teachers are able to check that learners have a thorough grasp of a word's meaning and identify any problems which might need clarification.

TASK 8 In 219, the teacher highlights the need for a specific piece of vocabulary (roller skates), which she then elicits from L6. She then emphasises the word (ROLLer skates) in 222 so that the whole class can hear. This is an example of scaffolding: the teacher 'feeds in' a new piece of vocabulary at the time it is needed. This 'linguistic support' helps the learners to say what they want to say and helps to maintain the flow of the discourse. In 227, she repairs an error (*went to roller skating) and models the vocabulary item for the class: *he went roller skating,* repeated. Modelling involves providing the correct pronunciation and form of the word for the whole class so that they can say it correctly.

TASK 9   Decisions concerning vocabulary selection relate very much to their usefulness, relevance and the extent to which they can be used in a range of situations. Depending on the group and their specific needs, appropriate selections can be made. A low intermediate group might usefully learn a fairly restricted number of chunks from this list (for example, *at the time, most of the time, this /that kind of thing, in the same way*), whereas an advanced group would certainly need to learn all of them over the course of time.

Chapter 6

TASK 1

In each case, the first sentence describes real, literal actions (*hitting a sack, having something on her hand, going to a wall*). The second sentences contain the same expressions, but the meanings are not real or literal – they are idiomatic or figurative (*hit the sack* = go to bed, *on the other hand* = a relationship of contrast between two ideas, *go to the wall* = go bankrupt, when a business collapses).

TASK 2

*I ran **to and fro** all morning.*   *You have to accept **the ups and downs** of life.*

These two idioms both consist of pairs of words connected by *and*. We call these irreversible binomials (binomial = 'two names'). They are irreversible because we can't say fro and to or downs and ups. Other examples include *here and there; fish and chips; safe and sound.*

*I will be **on hand** if you need me.*   *I'm **out of touch** with the latest pop music.*

These two idioms are both prepositional phrases. Other examples of prepositional idioms include *out of touch; in a fix; over the moon; under the weather.*

*I'm **ready, willing and able** to do anything to help.*   *They sold the company **lock, stock and barrel.***

These are irreversible trinomials. They are like binomials (see above), but they have three parts (tri- = three) instead of two. Other examples include *morning, noon and night; cool, calm and collected.*

*He's **as thin as a rake.***   *She was **as keen as mustard.***

These two idioms consist of comparisons with as ... as ... Other examples include *as blind as a bat; as strong as an ox; as heavy as lead.* They all intensify the adjective (*as thin as a rake* = extremely thin).
   This task shows that there is a variety of types of idioms with different forms.

TASK 3

A: *This economic crisis is terrible, everyone's losing money and people are losing their jobs.*

B: *Yes, and whose fault is it?*

A: *Well, it's the bankers and the politicians, but they never seem to take responsibility for it all.*

B: *Yes, that's right. They're always* **passing the buck!**

Speaker B uses the idiom to agree with A and to give an opinion which summarises the discussion. This is an extremely common function of idioms.

TASK 4 Learners might find both idioms difficult. Firstly, what do they mean? It may be impossible to guess just from context. Secondly, how formal are they? In fact, a shot in the dark (meaning a guess about something) is more neutral and less informal than put your foot in it (meaning to accidentally say something very embarrassing or inappropriate, or something which upsets someone). Another problem may be whether any variation is allowed: can we say 'a big shot in the dark'? – not usually; can we say 'push my foot in it'? – no. Another question is, are they both frequent, or rare, or old-fashioned? Is one more frequent than the other? A good idioms dictionary, or materials based on a modern corpus, will help answer these questions.

Chapter 7

Tasks 1, 2, 4, 5, 7 are dealt with in the body of the text.

TASK 3

Answers are underlined:

wet – <u>dry</u>, *light* – <u>dark or heavy</u>, *bright* – <u>dark</u>, *happy* – <u>sad</u>, *rich* – <u>poor</u>, *thoughtful* – <u>selfish</u>, *kind* – <u>unkind or cruel</u>, *give* – <u>take</u>, *blow* – <u>suck</u>, *push* – <u>pull</u>

TASK 6

a. Possible answers: *van, car, lorry* or *truck*

b. *vehicle*

c. Any two of: *van, car, lorry* or *truck*

d. *vehicle* is a superordinate of any one of: *van, car, lorry* or *truck*

e. *hatchback, saloon* and *coupé*

f. *car*

TASK 8

1 non-literal

2 literal

3 literal

4 non-literal

5 non-literal

6 literal

7 non-literal

8 literal

9 non-literal

10 literal

Chapter 8

TASK 1

1 'Her' in the second sentence refers to 'the little girl'. We know this from (a) our knowledge of the world (fathers pick up their children when they cry), (b) our knowledge of the language. 'Her' is a referent of 'little girl' and refers back to that noun phrase.

2 The events happened in the order they are reported. The two verbs in the simple past tense show this.

3 The other possible relationship is result: the little girl cried so the father picked her up.

4 We assume that the father is the father of this little girl, again based on our knowledge of the world and the use of the definite article *the* and personal pronoun, *her*.

TASK 2   There are several ways of doing this, here's one example:
I was born in Manchester, but spent much of my life moving from one place to another as my father worked in Manchester. It was surprising then that, after university, I spent many years living in the same part of the world, including Spain, Hong Kong, Hungary and Ireland. I am happy to say that, difficult as those times were, I am now back in the UK and happy to stay put – for the time being, at least!

TASK 3   *You know*, when you **hear** your **parents argue** you never **understand** why they're **arguing**, *you know*. Why do they **argue**? They have three great **kids**. *You know what I mean?* And, and then you *kind of* have to **realise** that, *you know*, they're just like any of us, *you see*. They have lots of **problems** and they have to **deal with** it, and it's **not so easy** to **deal** with them sometimes, *you know*.

The main topic of the text is 'parental problems' and there are several items in this lexical set which give the text internal unity (highlighted here in **bold-face type**). In addition, the speaker uses a number of discourse markers to create shared space where understandings can be established (highlighted here in *italics*). These words perform an important function, 'softening' what the speaker is saying and helping the listener to feel they're part of the discourse.

(1) The main topic is dancing.

> A: I think I could **dance** before I **sang**.
> B: Is that so?
> A: So I was like **four years old**.
> B: You don't keep it up, do you?
> A: **Dancing**?
> B: Yeah.
> A: Oh, I can get out there and **shake my boogie** if I want to.
> B: I'll **match** you any time, OK?
> A: OK. Sure.

(2) The main topic is car problems.

> A: That would explain why it's **stalling**. But it should **turn on** that **red warning light**, right?
> B: Um-hmm.
> A: Of course, it may not be **working**, but we know it **works** because it **goes on** when you **turn** the **key on**.
> B: Right.

TASK 5   The vocabulary items which help to create and sustain the topic are highlighted, all related to the theme of 'pot-luck suppers'. The topic switch comes in turn 48, rather abruptly: 'what adjective do we use ...?' The teacher could have marked this in some way with a discourse marker like *OK, right, so*, and so on. These 'signpost words' help learners understand what is happening and signal changes in topic or in a lesson stage.

45	T:	Oh dear, well, Georgia, perhaps when you go back to Italy, perhaps you can **organise** one of these typical **pot-luck suppers** and organise it, well, so you'll have plenty of **desserts** and plenty of **starters**, but do you think it's a good idea?
46	L:	Sometimes, yeah.
47	L:	It's nice because you don't know what you're going to **eat**.
48	T:	It's a **surprise** yes, yeah as long as you **like everything** ... I mean some people don't like certain things. What adjective do we use for people who don't like that and hate that, and a lot of food they won't eat ... we call it people are very ... FUSsy, fussy with their food. (*Writes on BB*) Right, so fussy, that's don't like vegetables, never eat pasta ...
49	L1:	Excuse me, how to say if you, for example, if you try some burger on corner ... on the, the street, and then you feel not very well.
50	T	Er ... I'm not quite sure what you mean, Yvette. If you ...?
51	L1:	You can buy, for example, just on the street.
52	T:	You mean street sellers ... people selling food on the street, yes?

TASK 6   *Underlined key lexical signals:*

A <u>textbook</u> usually consists of <u>detailed information</u> about the <u>subject</u> for learners who are studying the <u>specific subject</u>. It not only enriches the quality of the <u>language classroom</u> but also provides <u>clear structures</u> to <u>learners</u>, so that the <u>students</u> have a holistic view of the <u>lessons</u>. At the same time, it helps <u>language teachers</u> to carry out the target <u>language</u> (Nunan, 2003). Also, teachers can organise the <u>structure</u> of the language courses. As a result, using a <u>textbook</u> not only takes account of students' needs as <u>second language learners,</u> but also facilitates the learners' <u>learning processes</u>. (Cunningsworth, 1995).

An alternative version of the same text:
A textbook usually consists of detailed information ~~about the subject~~ for learners who are studying ~~the~~ a specific subject. A textbook ~~It~~ not only enriches the quality of the language classroom, ~~but~~ it also provides clear structures to learners, giving them ~~so that the students have~~ a holistic view of ~~the~~ lessons. At the same time, ~~it~~ a textbook helps language teachers to carry out the target language (Nunan, 2003). A textbook also helps teachers to ~~can~~ organise the structure of a course ~~the language courses~~. As a result, using a textbook not only takes account of students' needs as second language learners, it ~~but~~ also facilitates the learners' learning processes. (Cunningsworth, 1995).

TASK 7

1 Product information on the back of a moisturising cream.
2 Official letter from a property company.
3 Postcard.
4 Email from one colleague to another.

TASK 8

Sa-----tion: saturation, sanitation
Pro----ion: promotion, prohibition
Dis----ion: dissertation, discussion
En-----ment: engagement, enactment
Im----ity: immunity

TASK 9

The main problem with the vocabulary use in this short extract is that there are problems with the forms of words being used. For example, 'briefly discussion' (should be 'briefly discussing' or 'a brief discussion'); 'for teach language', should be 'for teaching language'; 'motivating' should read 'motivation'. Students need to be taught not only to choose the correct word, but also the correct form of that word for the particular context and co-text: where the word occurs in relation to other words in a text.

TASK 10

This is one possible version, there are others.
Holiday travellers faced long DELAYS today as French air traffic CONTROLLERS went on strike for the third day in SUCCESSION. At this busy time of year, the resulting effect was CHAOTIC. Many flights were delayed by up to six hours and some were even CANCELLED. Travellers were left STRANDED at airports and many were unable to leave owing to security regulations.

Possible strategies include: using world knowledge and familiarity with this genre of text (newspaper article); linguistic knowledge – *long* + noun, the collocation 'long delays', the phrase 'air traffic controllers', the verb endings *-ed*.

Chapter 9

Task 1 is dealt with in the body of the text.

TASK 2 (examples only)

im------ly:	immediately, immensely, immeasurably.
pro-----ion:	promotion, prohibition, promulgation.
un------ly:	unruly, unnervingly, unusually.
d-----ion:	division, depression, delusion.
i------able:	irrepressible, irredeemable, irritable.

TASK 3 Words which were unknown for me:
'two centre AO expansion', 'electron capture', 'Bohr velocity', 'pseudostates', 'bound states'.

Perhaps what's even more interesting is that there were many words whose meaning I DID know, but where it was still impossible to understand the text. This is due to a lack of world knowledge of the subject matter and highlights the need to start outside a text and help learners 'get into' it by pre-teaching vocabulary. Activating prior knowledge is central to helping learners understand or deal with unknown vocabulary.

TASK 4

pail	fail, sail, ail
pale	tale, ale, male
comb	tomb, bomb,
loan	moan, groan,
phone	photographic, phobic, phoenix

Note that it is certain distinctive features of a word which help us to associate that word with other, similar ones. Here, the /f/ sound in words like 'phone' and the silent /b/ in comb guide us to see words with this kind of spelling or sound.

TASK 5 For me, the process of association is something like this, though this may well vary from individual to individual and also depend upon cultural and educational backgrounds:

Cat	Dog (antonymy. In addition, these two words often collocate: cats and dogs, etc)
January	February (sequence)
Impossible	Possible (antonymy)
Table	Chair (association)
Bad-tempered	old man! (association and collocation)

TASK 6

to modernise or regenerate a town, city or residential area (gentrify)
a tool used for removing nails etc (pliers)
to disappear forever (become extinct)
a musical instrument, a little like a guitar (banjo)
part of a bicycle, used to change gears (derailleur)

TASK 7

- Reciting vocabulary from a dictionary (I: slow, time-consuming and a waste of time).

- Writing vocabulary lists in both English and the L1 equivalent (E: this may be useful – at least for low-intermediate levels, but it should not be the sole way of learning vocabulary).

- Recording new words according to their 'word family' (E: allows links to be made and patterns identified).

- Writing to a pen pal (E: good practice which forces learners to understand the importance of register, informality, idioms, collocations, and so on).

- Underlining every new word in a text and checking its meaning in a dictionary (I: we don't need to know every word to understand a text).

- Watching films which are subtitled in English (E: research shows that this is one of the best ways to develop a large vocabulary).

- Reading extensively in English (E: the relationship between reading and having a wide vocabulary is well-known).

- Listening to the radio in English (E: providing it is done actively and new words are checked or guessed from context).

TASK 8

Behaviourism suggests that habit formation and rote learning are essential to any kind of learning. Learning a language is another kind of habit formation, such as learning to walk or ride a bicycle. While this may be true to some extent, it is unlikely, in itself, to provide the kind of approach to vocabulary development needed for long term acquisition of a wide range of vocabulary. It would have to be supplemented by other strategies which rely more on the development of appropriate cognitive and interactive skills.

Chapter 10

Tasks 1 and 2 are dealt with in the body of the text.

TASK 3

Text message	Full message	What makes it more like spoken language?
Will b n twn l8tr. u on 4 it?	Will be in town later. Are you on for it?	Use of short forms, omissions of 'grammar' words (are, on, etc), abbreviated forms.
Thx 4 CD. C u soon ☺	Thanks for the CD, see you soon.	Omissions of article, use of letters which 'sound' like words: 'c' and 'u'
Hope ur feelin ok.	Hope you're feeling ok.	Abbreviated form 'ur', omission of 'g' in 'feeling', short form 'ok'
r u online?	Are you online?	Use of 'r' and 'u' as words.

TASK 4 Here are four ways of describing a dog. Why are they different?

canine mammal: formal 'scientific' description
dog: neutral, everyday usage
doggy: term of endearment ('nice doggy', for example)
bow-wow: register – used with small children

TASK 5 *Pavement* and *sidewalk* are synonyms; they have the same meaning. However, *pavement* is used in British English and *sidewalk* is American English, so there is a difference in geographical register. *Children* and *offspring* mean the same thing also, but *offspring* is a formal word which is typically used in written registers, such as fiction or poetry or religious texts. Once again, there is a difference in register, this time one of formality (formal versus informal) and mode of communication (written versus spoken). *Bolshy* and *difficult* are also synonymous terms which refer to a type of awkward and sometimes offensive behaviour, but *bolshy* is a very informal word which we usually only use in informal, casual conversation. All of these examples illustrate the trickiness for learners in using synonyms. There is so rarely a case where you can say that two words are 100 per cent synonymous in all varieties, registers and contexts. The learner has to learn about the different contexts in which each word is used.

TASK 6

1 Take two newspaper articles, one from a broadsheet like the *Daily Telegraph* and one from a popular daily like the *Sun*. Select one story which is covered in both papers and get students to highlight all the key vocabulary items and compare them. What do they notice?

2 'Genre shifting'. Get students to take a written text such as a job application, a letter to a pen friend, and so on. Their task is to 'shift' the genre. This will involve, for example, rewriting the job application as a job interview, but still using the same information. The letter to a pen friend could be re-written as a more formal letter to a potential employer, for example.

Review answer key and commentaries

Chapter 1

1 prefixes

2 openness   hopeful

3 You may see these compounds written as one word or two: cellphone; snowstorm; hilltop; keyboard; shoelace

4 c

5 dog 1

worldwide 2

unthinkable 3

boredom 2

6 *FBI, CIA, BBC, WHO* are examples of initialism.

Brunch, blog, motel are examples of blends.

Flu, gym, maths are examples of clipping.

7 ri̱di̱culous; ha̱ppiness; <u>bus</u> stop; out-of-<u>date</u>

8 a. F (different linguists have given different figures); b. T; c. T; d. T

9 Yes. One in ten words will be new, which is too great a learning load so, at this level, learners will need help from the teacher or from a dictionary or other resources.

10 Anglo-Saxon words are often more informal in register than Greek and Latin words, so the learner needs to be aware of register when learning new words.

Chapter 2

1 b

2 Possible answers:

fringe

Meaning 1: hair which is cut short and hangs over the forehead.

Example: *My fringe is too long. It's getting in my eyes.*

Meaning 2: an attachment to the edge of clothes or other objects such as curtains for the purpose of decoration.

Example: *The jacket had leather fringes.*

terribly

Meaning 1: used to give emphasis to the degree of something.

Example: *I am so terribly sorry but your room is not ready yet.*

Meaning 2: very badly.

Example: *My son has suffered terribly.*

key

Meaning 1: a piece of metal of a special shape that you use to open a door.

Example: *I put the key in the door and opened it.*

Meaning 2: the buttons on a keyboard

Example: *Press the delete key if you want to erase what you have written.*

light

Meaning 1: not weighing very much or less that you expected.

Example: *This bag is very light.*

Meaning 2: a book, music or films that is light, is one that is enjoyable but which doesn't make you think very deeply about it.

Example: *He plays light classical piano.*

3 homonym

4 Only b is true.

5 *hippy*

denotative meaning: *a term used in the 1960s and 1970s to describe people who dressed, behaved and lived in an alternative way and believed in peace and love.*

connotative meaning: (possible answer) *scruffy*

dove

denotative meaning: *a white bird that looks like a pigeon*

connotative meaning: (possible answers) *peace*

beach

denotative meaning: *a sandy area beside the sea*

connotative meaning: (possible answers) *holidays*

6   (Possible answers) <u>*Car, lorry, truck*</u> are co-hyponyms of *vehicle.*

(Possible answers) <u>*Bed, couch, table*</u> are co-hyponyms of *furniture.*

<u>*Hot*</u> and *cold* are antonyms.

Automobile and <u>*car*</u> are synonyms.

7   An example of a formal register: (possible answer) academic writing

An example of an informal register: (possible answer) an email to a friend

8   *Bait* is <u>food</u> which you <u>put</u> on a hook or in a trap in order to <u>catch</u> <u>fish</u> or <u>catch</u> <u>animals.</u>

9   Cognates are words which look the same in two or more languages and have the same or very similar meaning in those languages, for example *important* in English and *importante* in Spanish.

Advantages: where they exist and have equivalence, they make for very easy and immediate vocabulary building.

Disadvantages: they are very often pronounced slightly differently (particularly in terms of word stress) and they usually differ slightly in how they are spelt so this can lead to errors of transfer. Also, many words which seem to be cognates are in fact not and these lead to errors (we call these 'false cognates' or 'false friends').

10 Extensive reading and working with concordance lines accelerates vocabulary development because learners encounter new words and new meanings of words that they already know. The more they read extensively or do concordances, the more they encounter these new words and meanings and thus the more they increase the breadth and depth of their vocabulary.

Chapter 3

1   c
2   brown hair T
    a delicious house U
    to ride a car U
    beige hair U
    a delightful house T
    to ride a horse T
3   very good   weak
    auburn hair   strong
    utterly ridiculous   restricted
4   c
5

collocation	opposite
I prefer **dark** colours	I prefer **light** colours
She has **dark** hair	She has **fair** hair
I hate **strong** coffee	I hate **weak** coffee
There was a **strong** smell of petrol	There was a **faint** smell of petrol

6   a. F
    b. T
    c. T
    d. F

7   This student's English is correct, but she could improve it greatly by not repeating *very* so many times. We've suggested some alternative collocations (in bold).

'When I arrived I was <u>**quite/really surprised**</u> to see that the streets were <u>**rather** crowded</u>. It was <u>**so difficult**</u> to walk along Oxford Street because everyone was rushing and seemed <u>**terribly busy**</u>. I was <u>**utterly confused**</u> by the London Underground trains. The city is <u>**wonderfully**</u>

exciting, but I was **extremely** <u>nervous</u> all the time.'

8 A: Deductive: the students go from the general rule to specific examples

B: Inductive: the students go from specific examples to forming a general rule

9 A teacher can use flash cards with a word on each card and ask students to see which cards combine with which. Words which combine could be on cards of the same colour. Another visual aid is to use word-bubbles, where you can show which words collocate with a key word. For example, here is a word-bubble for make:

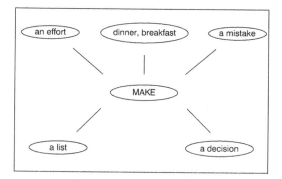

You can also use word-forks. Here is one for the verb do:

DO — your homework
/ your duty
a painting

10 A teacher cannot teach *rules* about collocation, because there are not any rules. Collocation is a relationship of probability: one word is more, or less, likely to occur with another. Students just have to learn collocations as they meet them. The most important thing to teach is *awareness* of collocations and why they are important.

Chapter 4

1 Colligation refers to how words form grammatical patterns with other words. For example, we use the grammatical pattern *go to* when we talk about going to a country (*I went to Ireland on my*

holidays) but we cannot say *go in a country*.

2 a

3 b

4 Possible answers:

a. A parent to a child: *Sit down!*

b. A boss to their secretary: *Will you fax this for me, please?*

c. A public notice: *No smoking*

d. A colleague to another colleague: *I'd be grateful if you didn't tell anyone about this.*

5 Mourn someone (He's mourning his wife.)

Mourn + for + someone (*I mourned for my dog Sam for weeks*)

Mourn the *-ing* of someone or something (*I mourn the closing of our local theatre*)

6 d

If a learning strategy is in place to focus students on these aspects of a word, then the new collocates and colligations will be easier to assimilate over time, as the word is encountered in new contexts.

7 Negative transfer is when the colligational pattern of a word is different in a learner's first language (L1) and this causes errors when they learn English because they automatically transfer the L1 pattern to English.

8 Some possible answers:

■ Consistently focus on the pattern of a new word rather than treating it as an isolated word.

■ Encourage your students to reflect on the pattern of a new word in their first language and to compare this with the pattern in English. Sometimes it will be the same but very often it will not.

■ Promote the use of vocabulary notebooks and develop strategies for note-taking that include colligational information about new words.

9 Dictionaries are particularly good, especially monolingual learner dictionaries. Gap-filling and cloze test tasks are also

very worthwhile because they focus students on patterns. Corpus-based tasks using concordance lines are also very useful.

10 If the corpus is appropriate to the level of the students, then they will be better able to understand the concordance lines and also the amount of colligational patterns will be level-appropriate. One way of achieving this is to use data from their readers or their own writing (always make sure that you have permission to use data in your corpus).

Chapter 5

1

Word	Root	Affix(es)
Photographic	Photograph (n)	-ic (adjective)
Countries	Country (n)	-ies (irregular plural)
Disappointment	Disappoint (v)	-ment (noun)
Redundancy	Redundant (adj)	-cy (noun)
Irrelevance	Relevant	ir- (negative); -ance (noun)

2 This is only necessary as a strategy when learners are trying to work out the meaning of a new word or when an explanation is given for a new word. Typically, learners should encounter words and learn them in their full form.

3 They are difficult to interpret as their meanings are not always literal; meanings cannot always be guessed from context; some can be separated from their particle, others cannot; they may have multiple meanings.

4 To go off: *to disembark (from a bus), to explode, to become bad, inedible (food).*

To get by: *to manage, to pass.*

To make do: *to manage, to tolerate, to suffer.*

To put up: *to erect, construct, to accommodate someone.*

To get through: *to succeed with difficulty, to pass (an exam), to pass (through a tight space).*

5 a. Correct. Chunks are ready-made and there play an important role in fluency as learners do not have to recall every single word.

b. Incorrect. Chunks may be formal (as in *to sum up*) or informal (as in *you know*).

c. Incorrect. Chunks often contain grammar words, for example *you see* and *at the moment*.

d. Correct. Chunks may have three, four and even five or more words.

6 Selection: according to the level of the class and usefulness of the chunk.

Frequency: use those chunks which occur most frequently.

Specific features which need to be highlighted in relation to form, function and pronunciation.

7 Unimportant: prefix *un-*, used to make a word negative.

Laughable: suffix *-able*, used to change the form of a word to an adjective.

Management: suffix *-ment*, used to change the form of a word, here to change the verb 'manage' into the noun 'management'

8 There are many, here are some examples:

Desk: desk-top, roller desk, desk clerk, desktop publishing, front desk.

Shoe: if the shoe fits, to be in someone's shoes, the shoe was on the other foot,

Cup: cup and saucer, cup-handle, cupboard, cup final, cuppa.

Tip: tip of the iceberg, tip of the tongue, tip over, tip up, tip-off.

9 Again, there are many, here are some examples:

Time	for a time, at the time, on time, out of time, in the nick of time, time after time, for time immemorial.
Way	change in the way, in the same way, out of the way, in the way, on your way, in some ways.
end	at the end of, in the end, at the end of the day, from beginning to end, at the other end.

10 *At the time; at the end of.* These are the only ones which are easily transferable to other contexts, which are transparent and which have relatively fixed meanings. The others either occur less frequently or are more open to interpretation from context.

Chapter 6

1 b

2 (b) Our plan **worked like clockwork.**

(c) **Give me a hand with** this box, please.

(e) No-one else had any money, so I had to **foot the bill.**

3

possessive	the cat's whiskers
binomial	down and out
verb+object	burn your bridges
prepositional	out of touch
trinomial	cool, calm and collected
compound	a vicious circle
simile	as dead as a doornail

4 b

5 eye ✔

hand ✔

cat ✔

6 a. F

b. F

c. T

d. T

7 a

8 a. F

b. F

c. T

9 a. They are often colourful ✔

b. They are often humorous ✔

e. They are often used to evaluate events ✔

10

journalism	business	computers	music
a last-ditch attempt	drive a hard bargain	one-click purchasing	top the charts

Chapter 7

1 *salmon*: *salmon* is a type of fish (hyponymy)

explore: *explore* means to *search* and *discover* (synonymy)

dry: *dry* is the opposite of *wet* (antonymy)

open: *open* is the opposite *closed* (antonymy)

dressing table: *dressing table* is a type of furniture (hyponymy)

2 bright – dark (antonyms); smooth – rough (antonyms); bear – bare (homophones); scarf, gloves, dress, shirt (co-hyponyms); sidewalk – footpath (synonyms)

3 Possible answer: *Can you chop a slice of bread for me please?* Students might mistakenly use *chop* interchangeably with *cut*. They are not 100 per cent synonymous. *Chop* usually refers to cutting something into small pieces, often with an axe.

4 False cognates are words that look and sound the same in two or more languages but which actually do not mean the same. One example is the French word *librairie* which sounds like the English word *library* but it actually means bookshop.

5 hyperonymy

6 A superordinate is a category word such as *furniture, meat, vehicles, clothing.*

7 Homophone refers to words which sound the same but which are not related in meaning, for example, *read* and *reed*. Homograph refers to words which look exactly the same and which are not related in meaning. Their pronunciation may also differ. For example *mean* as in *What does this mean?* and *mean* as in *You are so mean!* (nasty).

8 *nightmare, asleep, threw away, destroyed*

9 Possible answers:

Meaning: come together with people

Example: *We are going to meet Jane and Liam for dinner later.*

Synonym: join

Meaning: be able to pay a debt on time

Example: *The company isn't going to be able to meet its repayments on their loan next month.*

Synonym: repay

Meaning: sporting event

Example: *At the first meet of the season, Orwell ran his fastest time ever.*

Synonym: event

10 Concordance lines show the many uses of a word in context and they allow us explore the different patterns of collocational (what words co-occur with the search word) and colligational (what grammar patterns the search word has). It will also bring to light how words are used metaphorically.

Chapter 8

1 Texts have cohesion – sentences are tied together by cohesive devices, coherence – sentences follow each other in ways which make sense. Texts reflect real-world knowledge – we interpret them by using what we know about what happens in real life.

2 Lexical cohesion refers to the ways in which words give a text a kind of internal unity, a logical structure which helps to create understanding. For example, we may use antonyms and synonyms and words from the same lexical set to give a text its internal unity.

3 To what extent do **teachers of EFL** *hinder or facilitate* learner contributions by

their use of **language**? How can **teachers** enhance the *quantity and quality* of learner output by more careful language use? In what ways do **teachers** deny learning opportunities by *'filling in the gaps'* or *'smoothing over'* learner contributions? Adopting the position that maximising learner involvement is conducive to second language acquisition, this paper examines the ways in which **teachers**, through **their** choice of language, *construct or obstruct* learner participation in face to face classroom communication. (Walsh, 2002)

Internal cohesion is enhanced by careful vocabulary selection which helps to create a sense of topic and sub-topics.

Teachers of EFL (boldfaced here): teachers, their – all make some reference to teachers.

Learners (underlined here): learner output, learner involvement, learner participation, learner contributions, learning opportunities – all make some reference to learners and learning.

Key verbs: (italicised here): hinder or facilitate, construct or obstruct, filling in the gaps, smoothing over – these all make some reference to what teachers *do* through their use of language.

4 Lexical signals show a reader how different parts of a text 'hang together' and how they relate to one another. They 'signal' different aspects of a text and show, for example, how one part contrasts with another or gives an example of something said earlier.

5 Field: the subject and purpose of the message (for example, a newspaper advertisement for a job).

Tenor: relationship between the sender and receiver (for example, two colleagues, husband and wife).

Mode: how the message is communicated (conversation, telephone).

6 *Lexical density* refers to the ratio of unknown words to known words in a text. If the ratio is too high, for example, where 30 to 50 per cent of the words are unknown, learners will not be able to understand the text. One way of helping is to pre-teach some vocabulary items or to simplify the text by adding in words which are known to learners.

7 Inference is basically 'reading or listening between the lines'. We can infer meanings from context and we need to train learners in this skill so that they are able to cope with texts which contain unknown words.

8 Typically, we use linguistic knowledge about the form, meaning and use of vocabulary. We use knowledge of the co-text (surrounding words) and we use our own world knowledge.

9 Write a short text of around 50–60 words. Include 6–8 nonsense words.

■ What knowledge about words in texts did you use to 'create' these nonsense words?

■ choose words which have affixes such as *in-*, *pre-*, *-ation*, *-ess*, *-ic*, etc.

■ these affixes give us vital clues about parts of speech.

■ in addition, we use the 'co-text' – surrounding words to help us work out these meanings.

10 Devise one activity designed to help learners understand cohesion.

Task 2 in this chapter provides a useful model for writing an activity. As a first step, adapt this activity and then see how you might extend it.

Chapter 9

1 The mental lexicon considers the ways in which we collect, store, retrieve and make use of words in our minds. It is important in vocabulary learning as it offers some insights into the ways in which these processes are managed so that we can help learners acquire, retain and use vocabulary.

2 Knowing a word means knowing how to spell it, what it means, how to pronounce

it, knowing its word class and form, its derivations. We also need to know a word's synonyms and how it collocates with other words. In addition, we may need to know something about its register and connotations.

3 a. Input: the ways in which we are exposed to vocabulary in a formal, classroom context, or through our own reading, listening and so on.

   b. Storage: how we organise vocabulary in our mind, possibly best seen as a form of network or web in which words are connected to one another in different ways.

   c. Retrieval: how we recall words for use at a particular moment in time.

4 Devise a semantic network for 'weather'.

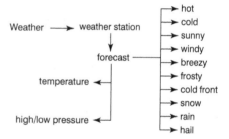

5 Helping learners to retrieve vocabulary entails verbally 'guiding' them. This might involve asking guiding questions, giving clues, asking another learner, using mime or facial expressions, using similar words (*it's a bit like X*), and so on.

6 Meta-cognitive strategies relate to the learning process itself. Helping learners develop better learning strategies is intended to help the learning process. Examples include: watching subtitled films, recording new words on voice-recording device, listing words according to their semantic fields, and so on.

7 Negotiation of meaning considers the ways in which new meanings are negotiated in the 'give and take' of classroom interaction. It is especially important to the acquisition of new words since this is

where meanings are clarified, adjusted and fine-tuned. Learners need to have such opportunities to clarify and check meanings if they are to really be able to say what they mean.

8. a. Scaffolding: refers to the linguistic supports that are given to help learners use a word correctly.

   b. ZPD: this is the difference between how far a learner can progress when working alone or with an 'expert knower' like a teacher. For example, learners would normally learn vocabulary when working alone, but would learn more and more quickly when working with a teacher.

   c. Form-focused instruction: this is when learners work together on some aspect of language; it may entail solving a particular problem.

9. If learners are able to store words effectively (for example, by using a range of strategies to record and learn new vocabulary), they are more likely to recall them as and when needed. Fast recall aids fluency, especially in speech, because there are fewer hesitations and interruptions to the flow of the interaction.

10. There are many, here are some:

   - Highlighting that a word needs to be replaced by repeating with a rising intonation, clapping (see example above), using facial expression, and so on.
   - 'Describing' a word without actually using it so that learners can try and 'guess'.
   - Simply inputting the word as and when needed – also known as scaffolding.
   - Using direct repair to quickly correct a word.
   - Involving another learner or learners to help a student notice an error or need for an alternative word.

Chapter 10

1. Old words (archaisms) disappear from use and new words appear in accordance with changes in technology, changes in society, culture, norms and so on; these 'new' words may be combinations of existing words or use existing words to represent new meanings (for example, 'greenhouse' in 'greenhouse effect').

2. Three from the following:
   (a) new combinations of existing morphemes
   (b) new combinations of existing words which make new compounds
   (c) words made up by other processes such as acronyms and blends
   (d) words borrowed from other languages
   (e) new meanings given to existing words.

3. These are suggestions only. Text messages are shorter, more informal and make use of various 'short-cuts' (*l8r*, *c u* and so on). Essentially, they are closer to spoken language than written.

Message	Text message
See you later.	C u l8r
I'll be arriving at about 10 am.	Arrive 10ish
I'm busy right now, I'll call you later.	Busy @ mo, call u l8r
I love you too.	Luv u 2

4. (1) Inappropriate response because it is far too long and too detailed.
   (2) We normally give a reason when we want to decline an invitation.
   (3) Too little information – we would normally add a 'softener': *yes, but do come in*, for example.
   (4) Sarcastic response, may be used as a kind of joke, but may also seem impolite.

5. Skinny: normally negative, but could be positive if used to contradict someone.
   Well-made: positive
   Lanky: negative
   Matronly: negative
   Long-limbed: positive

6 It's raining cats and dogs: *It's pouring down / throwing it down.*

How do you do?   *Hi. / Hello. / How's it going?*

He's an awfully nice chap   *He's a really nice guy / bloke / fellow*

We had a glorious time!   *We had a lovely / fantastic time!*

What a spiffing outfit!   *That's / What a lovely dress / skirt / suit.*

7 This is designed to teach learners that words have different meanings and can be more or less 'loaded' in terms of their meanings. The words in column B are more 'neutral', while those in column A carry more specific meanings which would only be appropriate in specific contexts.

Get learners to do the task in pairs, compare with another pair, add their own words and repeat. Finally, get them to summarise what this activity teaches them about the nature of words and how meanings vary according to contexts.

8 Get students to identify how lucky combines with other words (such as *really, very, flipping* and so on).

What words apart from nouns come after lucky (*to, that,* and so on).

Get students to produce a four-line dialogue using four different lines from the concordance lines and making other changes.

9 Possible answers: a) working with dictionaries to explore more meanings of words they already know; b) building up knowledge of compound words through dictionaries; c) using web-based dictionaries; d) developing good word-building practices as part of their vocabulary notekeeping skills; e) reading more and using dictionaries to explore new words or new meanings.

10 A = *blaze* (fire), *youths* (young people); B = *make an incision* (cut a hole), *recuperate* (get better); C = *grow the profit margins* (make more money); D = *conversely* (in the opposite way), *empirical* (based on evidence)

Glossary

acronym an acronym is a word made by using the first letters of several words to make a new word which we pronounce as a whole word. Examples include *Esso* (Standard Oil), *laser* (Light Amplification by Stimulated Emission of Radiations) and *radar* (Radio Detection And Ranging).

affix an affix refers to the additional elements which we add at to the beginning or end of a word. For example, the word *unproblematic* is made up of the root *problem*, the prefix *un-*, and the suffix *-atic*. By combining these various elements, we can change both the form and meaning of a word; in this case, from the noun *problem* to the adjective *unproblematic*.

anchor words these are the words in a text which have fixed meanings and which help to hold the text together.

antonym/antonymy/antonymous an antonym is a word which has the opposite meaning to another word. *Hot* and *cold* are antonyms in English. They are antonymous to each other. They are an example of antonymy.

archaism an archaism is a word or expression which was once used, but which is old-fashioned and not used any more in the language.

binomial English has a number of pairs of words which are fixed both syntactically and semantically; that is, both the word order and meaning are invariable. Examples include *salt and pepper, to and fro, over and over*. ⋙ **trinomial**

blend a blend is a new word formed from parts of other words. *Brunch* is formed from part of <u>*break*</u>*fast* and part of *lu*<u>*nch*</u>. *Motel* is formed from part of <u>*motor*</u> and part of <u>*hotel*</u>.

bottom-up if you process language bottom-up (for example, when reading a text), you try to decode it word-by-word, without considering the whole meaning. ⋙ **top-down**

breadth of knowledge breadth of knowledge means how many words and expressions we know. ⋙ **depth of knowledge**

clipping a clipping is a shorter form of a longer word which is normally used instead of the long form. Examples include *phone* for *telephone*, *gas* for *gasoline*.

cognate cognates are words which are similar in two languages or more languages because they come from the same source, for example *hospital, police, restaurant*. A false cognate or 'false friend' refers to a word that appears to be similar in form and meaning in two or more languages but is not, for example *sympathetic* is a word in English and in French it does not mean the same thing.

cognitivist refers to theories of SLA which argue that learning a second language is essentially a cognitive activity which takes place within the human mind.

co-hyponym when words share the same quality, we call them co-hyponyms, for example, *sheep, cows, horses, dogs, cats* are all co-hyponyms because they share the quality of being animals. ⋙ **superordinate**

colligation colligation refers to how words form grammatical patterns with other words. For example, the grammatical pattern *in the* is part of many patterns but not all. We can say *in the end, in the beginning, in the middle,* but we cannot say *in the start* or *in the day*. ⋙ **collocation**

collocation collocation means the way words combine to form pairs which occur frequently together. Examples of collocation include *make an effort, do one's duty, torrential rain, strictly forbidden*.

compound word a compound word is a single unit of meaning consisting of two or more individual words. Examples of compounds include *car park, desktop, waste paper basket, website, washing machine, brother-in-law*.

comprehensible input this refers to the words that learners are exposed to as 'input' when learning a second language. Many people maintain that this language should be at or slightly above learners' current level of English. ⋙ **output**

connectionism this is the theory which explains how words are stored in our mental lexicon. Connections in the brain between words are constantly made and re-made, strengthened and solidified. An understanding of this process is useful to both teaching and learning vocabulary.

connotative meaning this is the emotional or subjective meaning that we attach to a word. For example, *heart* means the organ that pumps blood around our body but it has a connotative meaning associated with love. ▶ **denotative meaning**

corpus/corpora a corpus (plural: corpora) is a collection of texts (spoken or written) stored in a computer, which can be searched to find out how language is used. Corpora often consist of tens of millions of words in different types of texts (e.g. novels, newspapers). Well-known corpora include the British national Corpus and the Bank of English.

data-driven learning (DDL) DDL is the use of corpus data directly in the classroom, where the students become researchers and work out for themselves how the language is used by looking at examples in the corpus.

deconstruct the ways in which we divide a word into its smallest meaningful parts (called morphemes) in order to understand its meaning: for example, *unproblematic* can be deconstructed: *un-, problem, -atic*. ▶ **morpheme**

deductive deductive learning means learning a rule, then applying it to new examples. If I learn the rule 'third-person singular present-tense verbs end in -s', and I see examples such as *takes, walks, laughs*, I deduce that they are third person singular present tense verbs. ▶ **inductive**

de-lexical verb a de-lexical verb is a verb which takes most of its meaning from the words it collocates with. For example, *get* means something different, depending on whether we say *get a newspaper* (buy), *get dark* (become) *get the phone* (answer), etc. De-lexical verbs include *do, get, go, make, take*.

denotative meaning this is the core meaning of a word; for example, the denotative meaning of *heart* is as a central organ of the body which pumps blood but can also be used connotatively to refer to love. ▶ **connotative meaning**

depth of knowledge depth of knowledge is how much we know about a word, for example, its different possible meanings, its collocations, its register, the typical contexts it is used in, etc. ▶ **breadth of knowledge**

derivation/derived form the process of making new words by using suffixes, for example, the word *beautiful* is a derived form of the noun *beauty*, using the suffix -*ful* to make an adjective.

direct repair this involves correcting an error quickly and simply without interrupting the flow of the discourse.

discourse discourse refers to any examples of language in use which is used to do something and which is produced in a real context.

discourse analysis the study of discourse.

discourse marker these are two- and three-word chunks which are used in spoken language to help create successful interactions. These include *I mean, you see, I see*, and *I know*. They function to help maintain the flow of a conversation.

form-focused a term used in the field of SLA to denote the extent to which a learner's attention is focused on the language itself. It is now widely believed that getting learners to focus on form is extremely important to their language development.

grade according to Stephen Krashen, it is important for teachers to adjust new language to the level of the learners they are teaching. Grading may involve simplifying language, using a more restricted vocabulary, speaking more slowly. ▶ **comprehensible input, lexical variation**

headword a headword in a dictionary is the word at the beginning of each entry, the word which the definition or explanation refers to.

homograph homographs are words which look exactly the same but which are unrelated in meaning (they may not be pronounced in the same way). For example *lead* in the following sentences *Maxwell took the lead early in the race, Lead is a very heavy metal*.

homonym this refers to words which have the same form but a different meaning; for example, *bank* can refer to the place where we put our money or it can refer to land at the edge of the river.

homophone homophones are words which have the same pronunciation but are unrelated in meaning. For example, *bare* and *bear, cellar* and *seller*.

hyperonymy hyperonymy refers to the relationship between a category word and a member of that category. For example, *vegetable* is a hyperonym of *carrot, building* is a hyperonym of *cottage*.

hyponym a hyponym refers to the relationship between a word which is a member of a category and the name of the category. For example, dog is a hyponym of *animal*, car is a hyponym of vehicle. ▶▶ co-hyponym, hyperonymy, superordinate

inductive inductive learning means looking at a number of examples of something and making a general rule based on them. If I see many examples of the word *as* after the phrase *the same*, I can induce the rule that *the same* must always be followed by *as*, not *than* or *of*.
▶▶ deductive

inference often referred to as 'reading (or listening) between the lines'. Inference refers to the ways in which learners *infer* meanings from contextual clues.

inflected form an inflected form is a form of a word which includes a grammatical ending to show person or number or tense. The form *reads* is an inflected form of *read*; the final *-s* shows that it is third person, singular, present tense (e.g. *he/she reads*).

initialism initialism is the use of the first letters (initials) of several words to make a new word which we pronounce as individual letters. Examples include *BBC* (British Broadcasting Corporation) and *CIA* (Central Intelligence Agency).

learning strategies the deliberate behaviours and actions used by learners to help them learn a second language. Examples might include listening to the news and writing down new words, keeping a journal, keeping an index file of new words, and so on.

lexical chunk a lexical chunk is a short phrase which is fixed or semi-fixed, and which we can treat as a single word. Because we treat them as single word items, they are quicker to learn and help to improve fluency.

lexical cohesion lexical cohesion refers to the ways in which words give a text a kind of internal unity, a logical structure which helps to create understanding. Lexical cohesion can be achieved by using words with similar meanings, words from the same or related word family and so on.

lexical item the basic unit of lexical (vocabulary) meaning. Many single words are also lexical items (e.g. *book, nice, catch, woman, flower*) but some lexical items consist of more than one word, they are multi-word lexical items, for example, *up-to-date, on the other hand, pick up, look forward to, bus stop*.

lexical variation a text's lexical variation refers to how many new words it has in relation to known ones. ▶▶ comprehensible input, grading

lexis another word for vocabulary.

mental lexicon the mental lexicon refers to the ways in which we store and retrieve words in the mind. An understanding of how the mental lexicon might work helps us understand how words are learnt and used.

metacognitive strategies these are the learning strategies used by learners to help them learn and remember new lexical items.

metaphoric metaphoric meaning is the opposite of literal meaning. *Heaped* is used metaphorically rather than literally in the following example: *Jake heaped four spoons of sugar into his porridge.*

morpheme a morpheme is the smallest unit of meaning. Words consist of morphemes. The word *car* has just one morpheme. The word *drinkable* has two morphemes (drink – able). The word *unthinkable* has three morphemes (un – think – able). ▶▶ deconstruct

negotiation of meaning a term taken from the field of SLA which looks at the ways in which speakers of a second language negotiate meanings by asking for clarification, confirming and so on. Some believe that negotiation of meaning is central to learning a second language.

noticing Refers to the extent to which learners are able to consciously take account of new language. Proponents argue that what learners notice is what they learn.

output this is a word used widely in the field of SLA (second language acquisition) to refer to the language produced by learners. Studying learner language can help us understand the process of learning more fully.
▶▶ comprehensible input

paradigmatically words can be related to each other paradigmatically. This means that they share a certain amount of meaning. The words *ignite* and *lit* in the following examples are related paradigmatically through the meaning of 'start a fire': *The fuel may have ignited in the heat, Grandmother lit the fire every evening.*
▶▶ syntagmatically

polysemy this refers to the concept that words can have many meanings, especially in different contexts. For example, *book* can refer to something that we read (*read a book*), it can mean to make a reservation (*book a restaurant*) and it be used in sport to refer to when a referee makes note of a player's name because they have committed some offence in a game (*book a player*).

prefix a prefix is a letter or letters added to the beginning of a word to make a new word. Common English prefixes include *un-*, *re-*, *im-*, as in *un*able, *re*write and *im*possible.

prepositional phrase these are multi-word units which usually comprise a preposition plus a noun phrase and often refer to place or time (for example, *at the end of the day, now and again, here and there*). They function as single word items.

procedural vocabulary procedural vocabulary refers to the words we use to describe and categorise other words. For example, *a type of machine, something we use to cook, a device we use to ...* Learners need to have a procedural vocabulary in order to understand definitions of new words.

productive knowledge productive knowledge of a word or expression means the ability to apply our knowledge of a word or expression appropriately in the right contexts, the right register, etc. ▶▶ **receptive knowledge**

productive use learning a word for productive use means not only being able to recognise it and understand it, but being able to use it correctly and appropriately when you speak or write. ▶▶ **receptive use**

receptive knowledge receptive knowledge of a word or expression means knowing whether it is common or rare or old-fashioned and knowing which variety and register it belongs to. ▶▶ **productive knowledge**

receptive use learning a word for receptive use means being able to recognise it and understand it in a text without necessarily knowing how to use it yourself. ▶▶ **productive use**

register this refers to how we use language differently in certain fields and activities depending on the formality of a situation, the age, gender, roles or relationships between speakers and listeners and readers and writers, or the professional context (business, media, academic writing). For example, we use certain language in formal letters (e.g. *yours sincerely*) which we do not use in emails to friends.

reiteration refers to the ways in which a word is used or explained in an alternative way. This is an important teaching strategy which is likely to be more effective than repetition.

salient if a word or expression is salient, it stands out in our mind, perhaps because we have met it frequently, or because it has special features that make it memorable.

scaffolding scaffolding is the process of providing linguistic supports to help learners express themselves more effectively. Typically, it involves a teacher 'feeding in' a new word or phrase as and when it is needed by a learner.

second language acquisition (SLA) refers to the process of learning a second language in either a formal (classroom) or informal (natural) context.

semantic networks refer to the networks we may use to store words. For example, if we take the word *holiday*, other words in that network might include *airport, passport, beach, suntan lotion*, and so on.

semantic prosody semantic prosody is the tendency of a word or expression always to occur in a particular kind of situation. The idiom *pass the buck* (meaning to pass the responsibility for something to another person) always occurs in negative contexts.

sense relationship this is the relationship of meaning that some words have with other words. Some words can have the same meaning (antonyms), some can have opposite meaning (antonyms), and so on. ▶▶ **antonym/antonymy/ antonymous, synonym/synonymy/synonymous, hyponym, co-hyponym, hyperonymy, superordinate**

signified a term used by de Saussure to refer to the mental concept that we have in our minds when we see or hear a word. ▶▶ **signifier**

signifier a term used by de Saussure to refer to the letters that make up the shape and sound of a word (or sign), for example, c-a-t /k{t/. ▶▶ **signified**

silent period when children learn their first language, they remain silent for quite some time and yet they are still processing and acquiring new language. Many people say that this is also true of second language learners and that all learners pass through a silent period.

suffix a suffix is a letter or letters added to the end of a word to make a word of a different word-class. For example, the suffix *-(e)r* makes verbs into nouns, indicating the person who does something, such as *read*er, *writ*er, *driv*er, *compos*er. Other common suffixes include *-ment* to make nouns (*government, commitment*), *-ful* to make adjectives (*beautiful, useful*).

superordinates a superordinate is a word which refers to a category, for example *animal*,

vehicle, building, vegetable, fruit.
➤➤ **co-hyponym and hyponym**

synonym/synonymy/synonymous a synonym is a word which has the same meaning as another word. *Start* and *begin* are synonyms in English. They are synonymous with each other. They are an example of synonymy.

syntagmatically words can be related to each other syntagmatically. This means that they are connected through syntactic or grammatical patterns. For example, the words *have responsibility* and *for* and *verb + ing* have a syntagmatic relationship in the following sentence *Liz has responsibility for locking the door every night.*
➤➤ **paradigmatically**

task-based learning which is organised around the completion of tasks is called *task-based learning*. The tasks are central to the learning process and the language used to complete a task should be almost incidental to task completion.

textuality the specific features of a text which give it its particular genre: for example, a newspaper article has a different textuality to a legal document.

top-down if you process language top-down (for example when reading a text), you process the overall meaning, rather than trying to decode each individual word. ➤➤ **bottom-up**

trinomial English also has a number of trios of words which are fixed both syntactically and semantically; that is, both the word order and meaning are invariable. ➤➤ **binomials**

word family a word family is a word and all its inflected and derived forms. *Start, starts, starting, started* and *starter* all belong to the same word family.

word searches this refers to the ways in which learners retrieve vocabulary as and when it is needed.

zone of proximal development (ZPD) this is a term associated with socio-cultural theories of learning. It is a metaphor used to represent the distance between what a learner would learn when working alone and what the same learner can learn with the help and support of an expert (for example, a teacher).

Index

Lightning Source UK Ltd.
Milton Keynes UK
UKOW07f0151121117
312539UK00004B/133/P